CONSORT

Graham and Heather Fisher's interest in the Royal Family dates from the time when they lived in Norfolk not far from the Royal estate at Sandringham, over twenty-five years ago. Since then they have written nine Royal biographies and many articles on the British Royal Family for major magazines all over the world. They have also collaborated on a number of novels.

Graham and Heather have been married for over thirty-five years. They have two daughters and three grandchildren. They now live and work in Kent.

D1329472

CONSORT

The Life and Times of Prince Philip

Graham and Heather Fisher

Star

A STAR BOOK

published by
the Paperback Division of
W. H. ALLEN & Co. Ltd

A Star Book
Published in 1981
by the Paperback Division of
W. H. Allen & Co. Ltd
A Howard and Wyndham Company
44 Hill Street, London W1X 8LB

First published in Great Britain by
W. H. Allen & Co. Ltd, 1980

Printed in Great Britain by
Hunt Barnard Printing Ltd., Aylesbury, Bucks.

ISBN 0 352 30835 4

Contents

Foreword

'The fact that I do not have to toe the party line is sometimes an advantage.' Prince Philip's words, meaning that because he is less constrained by royal protocol than the Queen, he can speak his mind more freely.

The fact that we have not had to toe the party line in writing this book – as it is not an official or approved biography – is, we hope, similarly an advantage.

Not that it is any the less factual or accurate on that account. Nearly thirty years of research, and of meeting and talking with people who have known Prince Philip at all the different stages of his life, have gone into it.

So many people have helped us over the years that it is impossible to list them all here and some, perhaps, would not wish to be. However, we would like to thank those who have helped with more recent research and checking, among them, Miss M. L. Currie, UK Executive, the Duke of Edinburgh's Award; Mrs P. Cary; Mr B. Hayward; Mr M. Keene; Mr John Dauth (Assistant Press Secretary to the Queen) and Miss J. Barratt.

In thanking them, we would make it clear that any opinions or interpretations expressed in this book, are – except where quoted to indicate otherwise – our own.

G. & H.F.
Keston Park,
Kent.

Curriculum Vitae

Name: Philip Mountbatten.

Style and Title: His Royal Highness The Prince Philip, Duke of
Edinburgh.

Height: 5 feet 11½ inches.

Eyes: Blue.

Hair: Blond.

Place of Birth: Corfu, 10 June 1921.

Father: Prince Andrew of Greece and Denmark (died 1944).

Mother: Princess Victoria Alice Elizabeth Julia Maria (died
1969), daughter of Prince Louis of Battenberg, later 1st
Marquess of Milford Haven.

Sisters: Princess Margarita of Hohenlohe-Langenburg; Princess
Theodora of Baden (died 1969); Princess Cecilie, Grand
Duchess of Hesse (died 1937); Princess Sophie of
Hanover.

Educated: MacJannet's School (The Elms), Paris; Tabors,
Cheam, England; Salem, Germany; Gordonstoun,
Scotland.

Naval Career: Cadet, Britannia Royal Naval College, Dart-
mouth, 1939; Midshipman — served *Ramillies*
(Australia), *Kent* (Indian Ocean), *Lanka* (Ceylon),
Shropshire, *Valiant* (Mediterranean), *Dryad* 1940–41;
Acting Sub-Lieutenant — *Excellent, Vernon, Excellent*,
1941–2; Sub-Lieutenant *Victory IV, Wallace* 1942;
Lieutenant — *Wallace, President, Excellent, President*,

[7]

Whelp (Home Fleet, East Indies, Pacific), *Victory IV,*
Glendower, Royal Arthur (Corsham), *President I,*
Chequers 1942–50; Lieutenant Commander *Chequers,*
Victory, Magpie, Victory 1950–1; promoted Commander
1952.

Naturalised British: 28 February 1947.

Married: Her Royal Highness The Princess Elizabeth (Elizabeth
Alexandra Mary Windsor), later Queen Elizabeth II,
elder daughter of King George VI and Queen Elizabeth
(now Queen Elizabeth, The Queen Mother) 20
November 1947.

Children: Charles (Philip Arthur George), Prince of Wales, born
14 November 1948.

Princess Anne Elizabeth Alice Louise, born 15 August
1950.

Prince Andrew Albert Christian Edward, born 19 February 1960.

Prince Edward Antony Richard Louis, born 10 March
1964.

Created: His Royal Highness The Duke of Edinburgh, Earl of
Merioneth and Baron Greenwich 19 November 1947;
member of the House of Lords 1948; Personal ADC to
King George VI 1948 (to 1952); member of the Privy
Council 1951; Admiral of the Fleet, Field Marshal and
Marshal of the Royal Air Force 1953; Prince of the
United Kingdom of Great Britain and Northern Ireland
22 February 1957. Granted precedence next to Her
Majesty 1952.

For major appointments, presidencies etc see Appendix IV.

Profile

Almost within hours of the official announcement of his betrothal to the girl who is now Queen Elizabeth II, Philip was thrown in at the deep end of royal life. A Buckingham Palace garden party seemed as good a place as any to put him on public display for the first time. Which may not sound so terrible, and in fact, isn't if you are a guest and can lose yourself among a few thousand others. But when you are on the receiving end of a laser beam of staring eyes, and unaccustomed to it, it becomes a very different prospect.

Not that it was Philip's first major royal occasion. There had been earlier ones – the coronation of the Queen's father in Britain and the restoration of the monarchy in Greece. But at those he had been no more than a very youthful extra. Even so, Greece especially, where restoration included the re-burial of Greek Royals who had died in exile, had been a strain.

Now, suddenly, he was no longer merely an extra, but the star of the show, the focus of all eyes. Tense with nerves he made his way through the excitedly chirruping crowd with his old shipmate, Michael Parker, lending moral support. No longer a Prince, having surrendered his Greek title to acquire British nationality, and not yet Duke of Edinburgh – simply plain Lieutenant Philip Mountbatten, RN, on around £11 a week – he wore naval uniform. 'Wellworn', some observers thought it.

'There is nothing the English enjoy quite so much as a royal wedding.' So wrote Walter Bagehot, the Victorian expert on constitutional history. A century later nothing had changed much and, if this wasn't yet a wedding, it was the next best thing.

The fair sex in particular wanted to get a close look at the bridegroom-to-be and it was easy to tell where Philip was as he grinned his way nervously towards the 'tea tent' or royal pavilion. It was where the parasols and picture hats were thickest.

Under the scarlet and gold canopy (a hand-me-down from the Delhi Durbar at which the Queen's grandfather, in the days of Empire, had been fêted as Emperor of India), King George VI sipped a refreshing cup of tea with an old friend. The friend made an appropriate observation about Philip's suitability as a royal husband.

'He's the man for the job all right,' replied Elizabeth's father, 'but I wonder if he knows what he's taking on. One day Lilibet will be Queen and he will be Consort. And that's much harder than being a King.' A century before, Queen Victoria's uncle, Leopold I of the Belgians, had sounded a similar cautionary note concerning Prince Albert. 'If he does not at the outset accept it as a vocation of grave responsibility, there is small likelihood of his succeeding,' wrote Uncle Leopold.

Victoria, of course, was already Queen when she took Albert to her bosom. For her great-great-granddaughter, at the time she married, monarchy was still in the future. So, for Philip, there were to be a few more years of freedom, a few years of coaching, before the need to step into his 'vocation of grave responsibility'. Just as he coached his elder daughter carefully and painstakingly towards her future role as Sovereign, so the dutiful and conscientious George VI, in the few years remaining to him, groomed his son-in-law towards his future position as Consort. And there have surely been times since when Philip, looking back, has acknowledged with a rueful grin that father-in-law was right: being Consort *is* much harder than being King.

Philip has been Consort since Elizabeth became Queen on the death of her father. Not Prince Consort. That is a title which has yet to be bestowed. And may not be. It was seventeen years before Victoria gave it to her beloved Albert following the birth of their youngest child, Beatrice. While Philip has already been married rather longer than that, it is, perhaps, not a title for which he is at all anxious. It smacks too much of Victorian times best forgotten; is too indelibly linked with that earlier Consort, his great-great grandfather, who was too staid and intellectual ever to be popular with his wife's subjects.

Philip has always been popular with the vast majority of British people. And still is, even if he is no longer the youthful Prince Charming of earlier days. The passage of years and the strain of the job have had their effect. Increasing baldness is nothing new. Like his father before him, he has been balding since his thirties. In those days he tried the sprouting possibilities of a restorative lotion, but quickly gave it up as useless. Short-sighted, again like his father before him, he has similarly been wearing glasses for around a quarter of a century, mostly conceal-ing the fact behind contact lenses or tinted lenses which might be mistaken for sunglasses. Today, even at the wheel of his car, he still prefers to keep his glasses tucked away until he is clear of the crowds.

Physically, he has kept himself in shape. He still carries him-self with naval erectness even if he is not quite the 'lofty six feet', 'over six feet', 'six feet plus' of popular legend. Five feet 11½ inches, in fact. Something of a keep-fit addict, he scorned palace elevators for years, preferring to skip nimbly up and down stairs, and if he is no longer as young as he was he still strides briskly ahead of his aides as though constantly on the verge of breaking into a canter. And if son Charles, in recent years, has shot out ahead in the Sexual Attraction Stakes, with his second son Andrew coming up fast on the rails, there are many women who still consider Philip attractive.

He is as much a workaholic as ever he was and hardly less active in his moments of leisure, even if, these days, he tends to tire more easily. But though he may sometimes flop out exhausted at the end of a long and tiring day, he does not really know how to relax. He continues to tilt at life as though deter-mined not to waste a single minute of it and, indeed, contrives to make a lot of minutes do double duty. He listens to the radio news while shaving and devours the contents of the day's news-papers along with his breakfast. In boyhood he was a bit of a guzzler, even to gobbling up what was left on a relative's plate;

inclined to plumpness until Gordonstoun took him firmly in hand. Elizabeth, brought up by parents conscious of the dangers of over-eating which constantly surround royalty, has always eaten more sparingly, and since marriage her example has rubbed off on her husband. So there is no porridge or cereal for royal breakfasts. Simply bacon and egg or a brace of boiled eggs with toast to follow. Keen to get on with the affairs of the day, Philip is not a man to linger over meals. 'It would suit him down to the ground if he could simply swallow a couple of protein pills and carry on working,' says an ex-palace servant.

Breakfast is often the last his wife sees of him until the evening. Indeed, if he is off on his travels – and he is arguably the most travelled man in the world, averaging 75,000 miles a year – it may be the last she will see of him for days. Charles, lunching with his mother at the palace on one occasion, asked if Papa would be joining them for lunch. 'Lunch,' sighed the Queen. 'If he takes on much more, he soon won't be here for breakfast.'

On those rare occasions when Philip is in for lunch, it is no more than a two-course meal. A main course of lean meat with a few vegetables and a side-plate of salad, with cheese to follow. No hors d'œuvres and no dessert. Dinner at the palace, if he is not out attending some evening function, is similarly short, though not sweet. No soup or hors d'œuvres. Again, a main course of meat or perhaps fish with vegetables and salad. No pies or puddings, calorie-filled cakes or sticky pastries to follow. Instead, another light savoury course with perhaps a few grapes to wind up. His drinking habits are similarly modest, perhaps a glass of beer at lunchtime, white wine with dinner, the occasional gin and tonic as an appetiser or whisky and water as a nightcap. His coffee usually comes black. He has not smoked since his marriage though in Navy days he was not above accepting hand-rolled cigarettes from shipmates at sea and favoured a pipe later. Like most reformed smokers, he abhors the smell of other people's tobacco. Hospitality requires that cigars and cigarettes are handed round to guests at royal dinner parties, but if the smell of smoking still lingers when Philip strides through to breakfast next morning he will order windows opened and send footmen scurrying in search of air-freshening aerosols. 'Let's get this bloody smog out of here.'

However late his return from some evening engagement, he likes to check his desk in case anything has come in during his absence. Once, with not long to go to Christmas, it was a batch of outgoing cards. Elizabeth had already signed them. A lot of men, after a hard day's slog, would have let them wait until the following morning. Not Philip. Painstakingly he signed the lot before going to bed – some six hundred of them.

'I am quite used to an 18-hour day,' he said once. But after fifty, 18-hour days take their toll and there are times, on a royal tour or at the end of a day of non-stop engagements, when it shows. His aides sometimes worry that he tries to do too much. If his work pace can hardly be said to have slackened much, it is slightly less frenetic than in his younger days. In those days, with requests to go here, there and everywhere streaming in at the rate of three hundred a month, he wanted to take on everything. It was clearly impossible even though he did once travel 1,500 miles to squeeze in thirty different engagements and make fifteen speeches in the course of a single week. Today, more sensibly, he limits himself to some 250–300 engagements a year, perhaps eighty of them involving speeches. Add on functions and travels he undertakes with the Queen and it still amounts to a substantial work-load.

He is, perhaps, lucky that his health has stood up to it. He has had his quota of coughs and colds; the occasional bout of jaundice. Nothing more. Which is perhaps as well in a man who regards ill-health almost as a weakness and dislikes it if people cough, sneeze or snivel in his immediate vicinity. If Philip is sometimes short-fused when healthy, he can be 'almost unbearable' when ill. Or so his wife was heard to say on one occasion. There was a weekend at Windsor when he went down with what looked very like influenza. He took to his bed, and Elizabeth, without asking him, sent for a doctor. 'Stay in bed and I'll call again tomorrow,' the doctor said, after checking Philip over.

'You'll call again when I send for you,' Philip rumbled, and on the following day, though still running a temperature, he not only climbed out of bed but insisted on driving back to the palace for work as usual.

In many ways, his role as Consort is an unenviable one. It poses, as he has said himself, 'lots of problems and difficulties.' That particular piece of soul-searching emerged on American television. 'Inevitably it's an awkward situation to be in. Still, you can get used to anything.'

It was years before Philip got used to it. Accustomed to running a tight ship at sea, to being skipper, he did not adapt easily or quickly to a situation in which his wife was his commander-in-chief. However much she contrived to defer to him in their private life – 'Ask Papa,' she would tell the children; 'I'll ask Philip,' she would say to friends – in the public arena, like a Japanese wife in reverse, it was necessary for him always to walk a few paces behind her; never to come between her and the limelight. Even in the tricky area where public and personal lives overlap, he had to settle for playing second fiddle. Because his wife was the Queen, their first two children were raised as Windsors instead of with their father's name of Mountbatten. Even later, when Elizabeth had a change of heart about this, the children did not become Windsor-Mountbattens, as they would have done in less regal families, but Mountbatten-Windsors.

The position of Consort is undefined in the British constitution and is, perhaps, indefinable. The natives of Papua New Guinea had it about right on the occasion they welcomed Philip as 'Number One Fellah Belong Missus Queen.' It is a part in the royal show for which no lines have been written and it was to take time before Philip settled sufficiently into the role to start writing his own. For a Consort there are no written rules and the unwritten ones tend to start with 'Don't'. Don't pry into the Boxes (those leather-covered despatch boxes which keep the Queen in touch with Cabinet and Commonwealth). Don't stick around when she receives the prime minister in audience (usually on Tuesday evenings). Don't upstage her in public. All negative; nothing positive. So the part of Consort becomes largely what the actor makes it. Philip has shaped it in his own image, non-stop, hard-working, outspoken, both prodder and booster of national morale, pricker of pomposity, patron of science, industry, technology. He used to be hot on education too, but has tended to steer clear since it became so much of a political football.

Like every other Royal, he is supposed to stay out of the political arena. Theoretically, he is barred from speaking on what he has called 'matters loosely-termed political.' It is not a rule he always observes even if his office, when the inevitable furore subsequently erupts, is quick to deny that he was in any way speaking politically. But by then Philip has said his piece, denouncing controls, restrictive practices, bureaucratic nonsense and so on. 'Over everything you try to do there seems to be a control or sanction.' 'If you ran a ship on a book of rules the whole time, with penalties and God knows what, you'd soon come unstuck.' 'This avalanche of lawlessness threatening to engulf our civilisation.'

If criticism is a sign of a job well done, then Philip has played, and continues to play, his part well. Prince Bernhardt of the Netherlands, the only other member of the Consorts' Union at the time, once advised him, 'It's a job for which you need the hide of an elephant. Everything you do will be criticised.'

Not quite everything, perhaps. But he has undoubtedly had more than his fair share of criticism heaped on him by politicians, parsons, trade unionists, conservationists, do-gooders. And not only in Britain. There have been anti-Philip outbursts from time to time in Australia, New Zealand, Canada, India, Italy and many other countries.

Victoria's Albert, in his days as Consort, had one major advantage over his great-great-grandson. He did not live in an era of mass communication. Victorian newspapers may have been more bluntly outspoken about royalty – certainly they were about the Prince of Wales who became King Edward VII – but fewer people read them. And there was no such thing as television.

Philip has made use of television in a way impossible to Albert but it has its dangers. Say the wrong thing and the whole world knows it within hours. Witness the uproar in Britain which followed Philip's comments on American television concerning royal finances and allied matters.

Where television points the way, newspapers are quick to follow. To the newspapers, the Royals constitute a real-life strip cartoon. And a strip cartoon, like a Hollywood western, must have its bad guys in black hats as well as its good ones in white ones. Otherwise there is no drama. The Queen, because she is Queen, is the No. 1 'good guy.' Charles, as heir to her throne, is another 'goody' (though he may not particularly care for the label). So Philip finds himself cast all too frequently in the role of 'bad guy'. Sometimes, for a change, daughter Anne gets the part instead. 'There are always people around waiting for me to put my foot in it, just like my father.' Daughter and father sometimes oblige. But at least Britain's newspapers stick to the facts on the whole. Some European publications are a lot less particular. As a result, Philip's marriage has been on the rocks, at least in print, almost as many times as he has had hot dinners.

If Philip sometimes seems to revel in the 'bad guy' image, there are other times when he has tried to duck it, redressing something said or done with a hurriedly-issued apology or explanation. Sometimes he has had only himself to blame that fur has started to fly. 'Dontopaedics' he calls it – or 'the science of opening your mouth and putting your foot in it.' And sometimes it is simply that he has opened his mouth at all. Left-wing politicians, in particular, often seem to be more incensed by who has said it than by what has actually been said.

Philip prefers his speeches to be 'interesting and constructive.' To do this without giving offence can sometimes be, he admits, 'a ticklish business.' His policy used to be 'when in doubt, play safe.' Judging by the content of some of his speeches in more recent years, he has moved rather away from that. His maxim for a successful speech is 'simplicity, humour, brevity.' He speaks sometimes from notes hastily scribbled while a meal is in progress, but where a major speech is involved prefers to write it out beforehand, then learn it off more or less by heart like an actor learning lines. He has always liked to write his own speeches.

[16]

'Boy' Browning, of Arnhem fame,* in the days when he was a royal aide, once tried to help out by drafting a speech for Philip. Pleased with his effort, he popped along later to hear it delivered. He didn't recognise the speech. 'There wasn't a word of mine in it.' He never tried drafting a speech for the Consort again.

Philip himself is often genuinely puzzled when he upsets people. In childhood, more than anything, he wanted people to like him, and still does. Under the skin he is a more sensitive human being than occasional public utterances and a sometimes abrasive manner on public occasions might suggest. He boasted around the time of his marriage that he had learned to read what was written about him with no more emotion than if he was reading about 'some animal in a zoo'. That is not always the case now, if indeed it ever was. Criticism can sometimes wound, sometimes anger, causing him to thump the breakfast table in indignation. 'Listen to what this bloody fool says here. . . .'

He is particularly hurt and indignant at anything which typifies him as 'an uncultured clot'. His own phrase. He thinks the image unfair. He is a man of more facets than most people realise. Over the years a picture has been built up of someone with more muscle than brain, for ever banging away with guns or slamming away at polo balls (at least, until he gave up polo). But there is more to him than that. He is also inventive, creative, artistic; model-maker, designer, article writer, oil painter, photographer. For examples of his photography see *Birds From Britannia*.† He has designed, among other things, a gift bracelet for his wife and the bronze fountain which stands in the rose garden at Windsor. The silver dog collar which became the Prince Philip Greyhound Trophy was his idea, as was the ingenuity of having a coroneted kangaroo on the gift cufflinks distributed to those who attended the 1968 Commonwealth Study Conference in Australia.

It was his idea too to put a changing selection of paintings from the Royal Collection on public display in what is now the

* Lieut. General Sir Frederick Browning.
† Longman 1962.

Queen's Gallery. He dipped into his own pocket to lighten the gloom of the Palace of Holyroodhouse in Edinburgh with a few more pictures by Scottish artists; commissioned the set of Coronation murals executed by Felix Topolski. The Arts Council, asked to advise on what fee he should pay Topolski, came up with a suggestion of £4.00 per square foot. Philip considered it degrading to an artist to pay him as though he was no more than a purveyor of floor tiles, four times 382 square feet equals £1,528. So he rounded it up to £2,000.

While he may not admit it, he is perhaps equally sensitive about gibes directed at his manhood, like the left-wing taunt in the House of Commons that he is paid by the state simply for being his wife's husband. Of course, a man with a stinging wit of his own must sometimes expect to be stung back. You can hardly expect to jest about a South American general's fruit-salad decorations – 'I didn't know Brazil was in the war that long' – without being subject to a rejoinder in like terms. 'At least I didn't get them for marrying my wife.'

Philip's own wit has become part of the royal legend. Like most legends, it has, perhaps, also become exaggerated. Just as a top comedian, at a dinner party, has only to say 'Pass the salt, please' to bring an outburst of laughter, so Philip's smallest utterance tends to become embroidered into a witticism, wisecrack, joke or jest. As a result when making a speech he is sometimes startled by an outburst of laughter where he least expects it.

He can indeed be witty, though his wit sometimes has a slightly acid quality. Or it reads that way later in print. As when a Borneo warrior, assigned to demonstrate the art of the blowpipe to the visiting Royals, huffed and puffed without any dart being forthcoming. 'Probably full of fluff,'' suggested Philip. Most people on the receiving end of such princely humour are usually too filled with awe to do more than give a weak smile or nervous titter in return. But the mayor of Calgary was made of sterner stuff. Philip, presented with the latest of several stetsons, traditional gift to VIPs visiting Calgary, moaned jokingly, 'Not another. Oh, well, I suppose I can always use it as a pot.' Later, the mayor also presented him with a magnificent spread of antlers. 'Don't ask me what to do with them and I won't tell you where to stick them,' he said, getting his own back.

Philip has his flaws, of course. As his aides know only too well, he can sometimes be liverish in the mornings. Judging by the finished portrait, his sittings for Annigoni must have been on just such mornings. The painting shows a stern, grim Consort. But true to life, say palace servants. 'Better watch it – he's wearing his Annigoni look today,' they sometimes caution each other.

The faults of 'impatience and intolerance' which his Gordonstoun headmaster, Kurt Hahn noted in schooldays, are still there, though better controlled, perhaps. There is also a stubborn streak inherited from his mother. Or perhaps it comes from even further back than that. Elizabeth has the same stubborn streak – so perhaps they both inherit it from Albert or Victoria – which occasionally leads to a clash of wills. Philip does not suffer fools gladly, hates wasted time or arrangements which are less than perfect, and can be short and sharp with those who ask what he considers to be stupid questions. Like the unfortunate BBC man, in Italy for a conservation conference, who had a message from head office in London asking the colour of the bears in the Abruzzo National Park. He popped the question to Philip at a press conference.

'Only such a mammoth organisation as the BBC could think of asking such a bloody silly question,' Philip told him. 'Tell your directors to go and look.'

He can be impatient with too much protocol or anything he regards as humbug. Excessive security used to irritate him, too, but these days, even if he still does not like it, he appreciates how necessary it really is. Handed a small package by a small girl during a Silver Jubilee walkabout in Perth, he made no attempt to open it but passed it to the nearest security man to be taken away for examination. It turned out to contain a bar of mint-scented soap.

Just as his wife has learned the art of hand-shaking without risking a crushed finger, so Philip has learned a few tricks of the trade of Consort over the years. Wherever he goes, whether to laboratories, factories or universities, he conveys the impression that he knows what he is talking about. And to a large extent, he does. 'He does not know a great deal about science,' said Nobel prize-winner Dr Edwin McMillan after meeting Philip in San Francisco, 'but he knows enough to ask the right questions.' That is Philip's main trick of the trade – knowing enough to ask the right questions. He has a naturally inquiring mind, not only for asking questions, but also for experiencing things himself. In his Navy days, wherever his sealegs took him, he would hire or borrow a car and drive out, sometimes several hundred miles, to explore the area in which he found himself and meet the local people. He has continued to add new experiences to his life throughout his years as Consort. He had already done some sub-aqua diving when he accepted the presidency of the British Sub-Aqua Club. Even so, he arranged for a leading expert to visit the palace and give him further lessons in the palace pool. Similarly, before opening the British Gliding Championships, he borrowed Peter Scott's glider and became airborne with a co-pilot to find out what gliding was all about.

He is not always so good at answering questions as he is at asking them and there have been occasions when the unexpected question has seen him looking flummoxed. Usually he tries to joke his way out of such situations. While this may raise a laugh from the rest of the audience, it does little to answer the question or satisfy the questioner.

Where Elizabeth is concerned, he has always been a helpful and protective Consort, cracking jokes to ease the tension when she is less than sure of herself (though this is less necessary today than it was once), plugging gaps in the conversation, displaying indignation or anger if he thinks she is being imposed upon. 'You can't expect the Queen to suffer this glare,' he rapped out in Australia when he saw the lighting which had been installed to enable her opening of Parliament to be filmed. He can be thoughtful and considerate of others too, quick to seize the hand of some nervous youngster who is uncertain whether or not it is correct to shake hands. Others might laugh when a woman, delivering an inexperienced curtsey, overbalanced in the act, but not Philip. He scowled at those laughing and subsequently sought out the woman to talk to her. An echo there of the Salem schoolboy who, when another boy had his head shaved for refusing to give the Nazi salute, sought him out and lent him a cricket cap to cover his skinhead.

His wife loves him and has done so since almost their first meeting. His children are devoted to him. 'A wise father,' Charles has called him, which may be overstating it somewhat, but certainly he has always done what he felt was best for the children. Sending Charles to Dad's old schools may have seemed a mistake to some at the time – and certainly Charles thought so – but has turned out well. Charles himself is the proof.

His aides admire and respect him. They know that his bark is worse than his bite. For his part, he knows his own faults. If he is sharp or sulky with those who work for him, invariably he regrets it later and does his best to make amends. He may not actually apologise, but he comes close.

His years as Consort have not been all hard work and no thanks, of course. Much of it has been interesting, pleasurable and exhilarating; if only because he is a man who delights in hard work and fresh experiences. Nor is it without its material rewards. Early naval pay of around £11 a week had become a state allowance of £135,000 a year by 1980. Of course it is not all pocket money by any means, as we shall consider presently. But he isn't short of cash. He has cars and aircraft at his instant disposal, horses and carriages at the ready for the new sport of carriage driving which he has taken up since synovitis of the wrist brought polo-playing days to an end, an extensive wardrobe of suits and uniforms, and a brace of valets to take care of them for him. So it can't be all bad, as Philip himself realises.

One of his guests on a royal occasion was Donald MacJannet, the American principal of the kindergarten in Paris which was the first school Philip ever attended. In those days he went to school in clothes which were sometimes patched, had to stay behind on one occasion because it was raining and he did not own a raincoat, and had to save for ages in order to buy his first bicycle. Meeting his old headmaster again all those years later,

Bloodline

Like his own son Andrew, Philip was an afterthought baby, conceived while his parents were exiled in Switzerland, born—on the Ionian island of Corfu—seven years after the youngest of his four sisters; a Prince of Greece without a drop of Greek blood in his veins.

Two ancient bloodlines meet and mingle in him. On his father's side he comes from the Danish royal house of Schleswig-Holstein-Sonderburg-Glücksburg* which, in the days when monarchs ruled as well as reigned, supplied not only Denmark with its kings, but exported them also to Greece, Sweden, Norway and Russia. On his mother's side he is descended from the Mountbattens,* who were Battenbergs until they changed the family name at the same time that King George V was changing his and can trace their lineage back through some forty-four generations to approximately 600 AD. He also has some English blood from Queen Victoria and a dash of the Russian Romanov. But not a drop of Greek.

This curious state of affairs has its origin in the days when Greece threw off the Ottoman yoke under which it had languished for centuries and established itself again as an independent kingdom. A kingdom needs a king, of course, but Greece had no royal family. Prince Otto of Bavaria was imported to start one, but did not run the country to everyone's satisfaction and was sent into exile, the start of what was to become an old Greek custom. Queen Victoria's second son, Alfred, was invited to take

* Appendices I and II.

[23]

his place, but his mother wouldn't let him. The job went instead to Prince William of Denmark, whose sister had recently married the future King Edward VII. He obligingly changed his name to that of Greece's patron saint and became King George I, only to be assassinated at the 1913 parade held in Salonika to celebrate another victory over the Turks.

Whilst all this was happening in Greece, elsewhere in Europe Prince Alexander, younger brother of the Grand Duke of Hesse-Darmstadt, was contriving a runaway marriage with a girl named Julie von Haucke. The Grand Duke was furious. Marrying a mere maid-of-honour, and an orphan at that! It was seven years before he forgave the runaway lovers and bestowed titles on their children, one of whom thus became Prince Louis of Battenberg. More than anything, young Louis, in boyhood, wanted to go to sea. But there was, at that point in history, only one navy worthy of the name – Britain's Royal Navy. So, just as William of Denmark became George I of Greece, Louis of Battenberg switched his German nationality to British in order to join the Royal Navy.

George I of Greece married the teenage Grand Duchess Olga of Russia, fathering two daughters and five sons, one of whom was Prince Andrew, Philip's father. Prince Louis married his cousin, Princess Victoria of Hesse, one of Queen Victoria's many grandchildren. They had four children, the eldest of whom was christened Victoria after great-grandmama but thereafter known as Alice to avoid confusion at a time when so many Victorias abounded. Alice was Philip's mother. She and Andrew were married in Darmstadt, the family home of the Battenbergs, in 1903. He was a tall, dashing, monocled cavalry officer. She was eighteen and very pretty, but afflicted with congenital deafness which was to worsen with the years. They had two daughters in quick succession and two more a few years later.

Andrew's brother, Constantine, took over the throne on the assassination of their father. Unfortunately for him, Constantine was married to a sister of the German Emperor, a fact which did not go down too well with Britain and France as the First World War ran its bloody course. So they intervened to depose him and installed his second son, Alexander, in his place. They felt that the eldest son, another George, was too tainted with his mother's German blood. The rest of the family, including Andrew, Alice and their four daughters, were sent into exile in Switzerland, where they lived on borrowed money, attended by servants who loyally went without pay.

They might well have stayed in Switzerland, and Philip might have been born there, but for another strange twist of fate. In 1920, Alexander, a king who was virtually a prisoner in his own palace, was bitten by a pet monkey. Blood poisoning set in and he died in agony. To the fury of Britain and France, a plebiscite in Greece favoured recalling the exiled Constantine as king. So back they all went, including Andrew and Alice, now pregnant again.

Not that Andrew saw much of his native Greece. They were hardly back before he was again in uniform, commanding an infantry division and later an army corps, as the Greeks swept into Asia Minor to do battle once more against their ancient enemy, the Turks. Philip was born in his absence, on 10 June 1921, on Corfu, in a royal villa with the curiously suburban name of *Mon Repos*. A local doctor effected delivery on the dining room table. He was born a Prince of Greece, sixth in line of succession to the throne. If this seems rather far down the list – Princess Margaret has a corresponding position in Britain today – it was not necessarily so in a country where a man could be king one day and an exiled nobody the next, and his mother, at least, nurtured a faint hope that he might one day end up as King Philippos.

In Asia Minor the dream of a new Greek empire turned to ashes. The Greek army was routed with the loss of some 40,000 men. Defeat on this scale always requires scapegoats and so Constantine found himself deposed for the second time, with his eldest son, whose tainted German blood was no longer of importance, installed in his place as King George II. But the real power in the land was wielded by a revolutionary junta headed by Eleutherios Venizelos, for all that he was not actually in the country at the time.

Philip's father returned from the wars to his island home of

Corfu, whence he was unexpectedly summoned to Athens. He journeyed there in the naïve belief that he was required only to give his own first hand account of the Greek tragedy enacted in Asia Minor and might possibly have to resign his commission. Instead, he found himself imprisoned on charges of disobedience and desertion. Philip's mother, as soon as she learned what had happened, appealed to her nephew, the King. But there was nothing poor George II could do. Like his brother before him, the ill-fated Alexander, he was a virtual prisoner in his own palace.

Like all revolutionaries, the Greek junta, on whatever pretext, needed to get rid of those who might oppose it. The Asia Minor debacle provided as good an excuse as any. In double-quick time an uncertain number of possible opponents were ushered in front of a firing squad. Most authorities agree on six – three ex-premiers, two former government ministers and the army commander in chief – but Philip's uncle, Prince Christopher,* says seven in his *Memoirs*, though he names no names. Whatever the number, there was a better than evens chance that the luckless Andrew would shortly go the same way.

Realising that no help was likely from her nephew, the King, Philip's mother looked further afield. She appealed to the Pope to intervene to save her husband's life, to the King of Spain, the President of France and Britain's King George V, to whom she was related.* Her appeal to George V was underlined by her brother, the young Louis Mountbatten, at that time a close friend of the King's eldest son, the Prince of Wales. George V intervened to play the sort of hand kings could still play in the 1920s and, in consequence, Commander Gerald Talbot was despatched from Geneva to Athens to negotiate Andrew's release or, if that didn't work, to somehow rescue him from prison. Talbot's was a cloak-and-dagger operation which, if it lacked an actual cloak and dagger, did involve a disguise and false papers. He arrived in Athens only forty-eight hours before the date set for Andrew's trial. In the meantime, Philip's mother had also

* Appendix II.

journeyed to Athens to be near her husband. Somehow Talbot managed to get to Theodoros Pangalos and Colonel Plastires, the two most important revolutionaries actually on the spot at the time, and a deal was done. Instead of being sentenced to death, Andrew was stripped of his nationality and military rank and set free.

It is curious how family history was to repeat itself. Louis Mountbatten had already embarked on the naval career which he was to see as a vindication of his father, unjustly hounded from office as Britain's First Sea Lord during the First World War because of his German connections. Similarly, the baby Philip, in the years ahead, was to achieve a status which he may also see as a vindication of the injustice done to his father.

It might have been worse. But for Philip's mother, her Mountbatten brother, King George V and Gerald Talbot, Andrew might have been executed. As it was, the revolutionary Pangalos personally drove him and Talbot to the quayside where the British cruiser *Calypso* was waiting with Alice on board. From Athens the cruiser headed for Corfu to pick up the couple's four young daughters and baby son. Philip was only eighteen months old, too young for a bunk or naval hammock. So the ship's carpenter set to work to fashion him a padded cot from an old orange box for the voyage to Brindisi.

Parisian Exile

For Philip, this was to be his first experience of exile – although he was obviously too young to think of it in those terms. It was different for the rest of the family. They had been in exile before. For Philip's father, in particular, that second spell of exile was a bitter and humiliating experience. The injustice of his sentence rankled and, stripped of his nationality, he was a man without a country. His relative, King Christian X of Denmark, later arranged for him to be given a Danish passport, but it wasn't the same. He thought of himself as Greek. Outwardly, during those years of exile, Andrew remained his old, bantering self, but inside him something had gone. Other exiled Greek Royals might nurture hopes of one day returning to Greece or dream of restoring the Greek monarchy. Andrew drifted into a life of easy pleasure, as far as funds would permit, first in Paris and later further south on the French Riviera. So a broken home was added to all the other uncertainties of Philip's young life. Yet today he does not look back upon those years of boyhood as being either unhappy or unsettled, maybe because he was away at boarding school for much of the time. Furthermore he retains fond memories of the father he was to see so seldom during his adolescence.

From Brindisi the family first made their way to Britain where Alice had so many relatives. Philip and his four sisters, with their English nanny, Miss Roose, stayed for a time with their widowed Battenberg grandmother, the Dowager Marchioness of Milford Haven, in her apartment at Kensington Palace in London while their parents journeyed to America to discuss things with

Andrew's brother, Prince Christopher, who had married the wealthy Nancy Leeds, widow of an American millionaire. Another brother, George, had also married well. His wife was Princess Marie Bonaparte who inherited a fortune from the grandfather who founded the Monte Carlo casino – and it was thanks to him that they were shortly able to move into a staff lodge on his estate at St Cloud in Paris.

Paris in the early 1920s was a bohemian city of exiles. The poorer ones scratched a living as best they could, working as seamstresses, laundresses, as drivers, in restaurants. The Greek Royals were not quite reduced to that, though another of Andrew's brothers, Prince Nicholas, augmented what little money trickled through to him from Greece by giving painting lessons while his daughter, Princess Marina, later to marry the Duke of Kent, quickly became adept at running up her own clothes. For a time, in a somewhat similar fashion, Philip's mother helped to run a shop in the Faubourg St Honoré, though the small profits derived from selling Greek artwork and embroideries would appear to have gone to charity rather than to meet family living expenses. Where the family's own money came from is not clear, but there appears to have been sufficient of it to keep Miss Roose on for a time, for Prince Andrew to eat in the best restaurants upon occasion and even to take off to St Moritz or Monte Carlo if the mood came upon him.

They were, therefore, not exactly on the breadline. Yet, equally, there appears to have been some embarrassment over the matter of fees when the question of sending Philip to school first cropped up. Donald MacJannet, the American graduate who ran the school, obligingly waived any question of fees. The school he had founded in a rambling old mansion called The Elms, originally intended for the offspring of the American diplomats and businessmen posted to Paris, was only a few blocks from where the exiled Greek Royals were living. MacJannet came to know the family and took a liking to Philip, a flaxen-haired spritely little imp with a likeable nature. Just as Philip, years later, was to feel that his son Charles was being spoiled by the cloying petticoat government of the royal nursery, so MacJannet saw Philip as a child whose natural liveliness was stifled through living in a household composed largely of women, mother, sisters and a nanny. So, even if he did not put things quite so bluntly as that, he pushed the idea that Philip would benefit from mixing more with other children of his own age and Philip started school.

Brought up to think of himself as 'Prince Philip', that was the name he wrote laboriously on his school books. Aged six at the time, he took to school life as a duck to water. An American who was at school with him remembers, 'He would get to school ahead of the other kids of a morning so that he could help give out books, fill the inkwells and suchlike. After school he would stay behind to clean the blackboard and help tidy up.' Then, as later, he was 'always on the go; he never seemed to stop'.

He was sent to school in clothes which, though clean and neat, were sometimes patched, sometimes darned. And there was one occasion when he stayed on at school even after all the helping-out had been done. He was waiting for the rain to ease. 'I don't have a raincoat,' he told MacJannet. 'But I'm expecting some birthday money from one of my uncles and I'll get one out of that.'

'You'll be able to get a good one,' MacJannet suggested.

Philip shook his head. 'I want to get a bicycle as well,' he said.

The uncle in question was Gustav VI of Sweden whose wife, Louise, was Alice's sister. It was a strangely mixed upbringing for a small boy, sometimes royal, sometimes almost threadbare. There were holidays with royal relatives on the shores of the Baltic and the Black Sea; other less regal holidays with the Foufounis family, friends of his parents. At the Foufounis' farm near Marseilles he helped feed the hens and clean out the pigs. At their holiday home near Le Touquet, in company with the small son of the house, he dragged out a couple of Persian carpets and went from door to door trying to sell them. Fortunately, the carpets were retrieved before a deal could be completed.

Other children thought him something of a show-off, standing on his head when visitors came to call, jumping off hay wagons and tight-roping along the top bar of the hurdles which enclosed the pigs. He once fell in the pig muck while doing this and jumping off a hay wagon cost him a front tooth. He was nervous of horses when he was first introduced to them, but always completely at home in the sea. He ran the gamut of childhood emotions, sometimes hungry for affection (some people thought), sometimes mischievous, sometimes pugnacious. He climbed trees, drove farmcarts as though they were chariots, once let the pigs loose on the afternoon of an outdoor tea party, scattering tables, tea things and visitors. And he once ran home from school in Paris proudly displaying the beginnings of a black eye. He had given the other boy *two* black eyes, he told his sisters.

Mixing with so many American youngsters at the MacJannet school resulted in him speaking English with something of an American accent. He learned American football chants and played baseball instead of cricket. But all that changed when the Mountbatten connection took over the shaping of his young life.

Schooldays

In the public mind it is the late Earl Mountbatten who is most closely identified with Philip's youthful upbringing. Confused by the fact that Philip later adopted the Mountbatten name and by the look-alike appearance of uncle and nephew, some people even think that Philip is Mountbatten's son. Though an almost father-son relationship was eventually to develop between 'Uncle Dickie' (so-called to avoid confusion with his father, Prince Louis) and his nephew, it was the elder of the two Mountbatten brothers, George, successor to his father as Marquess of Milford Haven, who was responsible for his sister's young son first coming to live in Britain.

George had earlier followed his father into the Royal Navy, taking part in the Battle of Jutland during the First World War, but by 1930 he was back in civvy street, a director of Marks and Spencer and a member of the New York Stock Exchange, among other things. His own son David was already a boarder at what is now known as Cheam School — it was Tabors in those days, though located at Cheam in Surrey — and generously he offered to pay for his sister's son to go there too.

Schooldays at Cheam marked the beginning of a close friendship with the slightly older David which was to continue into young adulthood. It was close enough for Philip to have David as his best man when he married, but was cooled following his cousin's published revelation of a stag party the night before the wedding and a suggestion that Philip might have had something of a slight hangover on his wedding morning.

But all that was a long way in the future during the days of boyhood. The atmosphere at Cheam was very different from what Philip had known at the MacJannet school in Paris; very English. Cricket in place of baseball and soccer yells instead of American-style football chants. Philip played cricket for the school, though only in the second XI. He won the school diving competition – he was always like a fish in the water – and tied for first place in the high jump. He learned to box. Academically, he shone at French, which was perhaps no more than to be expected of a boy who had been brought up in Paris, and at history.

Holidays were spent sometimes with his maternal grandmother in her rather threadbare apartment at Kensington Palace, where he was once caught by the police in the act of scaling the roof, sometimes at David's home, Lynden Manor, and sometimes with other relatives in various parts of Europe. But soon there was no longer a home in Paris to visit. Within the short space of two years his sisters were all married to German princelings. Sophie, the youngest, was the first to marry. She was only sixteen when she became the bride of Prince Christopher of Hesse, later to be killed while flying with the Luftwaffe in World War II. Cecilie, at twenty, married George, Grand Duke of Hesse, Margarita married Prince Gottfried of Hohenlohe-Langenburg and Theodora married Berthold, Margrave of Baden. His daughters married and off his hands, Prince Andrew saw no reason preventing him from drifting south to the pleasures of Monte Carlo. Philip's mother, in poor health, followed her daughters to Germany for a time, later returning to Greece, and the home in Paris was no more.

A youngster living at home might have found the break-up traumatic. Philip was not unduly unsettled. There was too much to occupy him at Cheam; too much fun to be enjoyed with cousin David. An old barn at Lynden Manor became an improvised amphitheatre for boisterous games of roller-skate hockey and bicycle polo. One roller-skating episode cost Philip another tooth. There was the river down which they could canoe to climb onto the roof of the Hotel de Paris and listen to the jazz band through the skylight. There was, on one occasion, a cycle trip to a

Scout camp at Dover and the return journey on a barge with two nights spent sleeping on grain sacks.

The one decision that upset Philip most about the family break-up was that he should transfer to Salem. He still had a year to go at Cheam and was happy there. But sister Theodora was married to Berthold, Margrave of Baden, and Berthold was now headmaster of Salem, an elitist school housed in a group of ancient monastic buildings on the shore of Lake Constance. The school had been founded by Dr Kurt Hahn under the patronage of Berthold's father, Prince Max of Baden. But Hahn was no longer around when Philip went there in the early 1930s. The Nazis had come to power in Germany and saw Salem, if its emphasis on leadership through service could be bent just a little, as being in accord with their ideas of a Teutonic master-race. Hahn did not agree, but the Nazis were not about to let that stand in their way. He was Jewish and so it was an easy matter to arrest him as 'an enemy of the State'. It was fortunate for Hahn that, like Philip's father before him, he had friends in high places. They managed to get him released and he fled to Britain, where his educational ideas became the springboard for another school started in another set of decrepit buildings, Gordonstoun.

Philip was hardly at Salem long enough to get his bearings and did not particularly care for the place. The curriculum, he found, was unorthodox by Cheam standards. The school day started with a cold shower, whatever the weather, to damp down the libido, a quarter-mile run to shake up the liver and domestic chores to induce humility. Following lunch there was a compulsory rest period when the boys lay on their beds while the masters read good works to them. Athletic pursuits included two classical Greek pastimes new to Philip for all that he was born in Greece; throwing the javelin and hurling the discus. He was quickly adept at both.

He was also adept at giving a mocking Nazi salute whenever he wanted to leave the room, and in Britain it would have been no more than good, clean, schoolboy fun. In Nazi Germany that sort of thing was highly dangerous, and not only to Philip. 'We thought it wiser all round if Philip left Germany,' one of his sisters, Margarita, revealed later. So Philip followed Kurt Hahn to Gordonstoun, on the shore of the Moray Firth. Before going there, however, there was a brief holiday at Cromer where he presented the prizes at a gymkhana organised by the Norfolk Riding School, which constituted his first public function.

Gordonstoun in the 1930s, was a long way from being the sort of educational establishment it has since become. It was then a small, all-male (it is now co-educational), tightly close-knit community of some thirty boys and a handful of masters. It had no playing fields and various buildings were still in the course of repair and conversion. An old stable was being adapted to serve as a dormitory. It fitted in well with Hahn's educational ideas that boys and masters should share not only lessons, but also such tasks as mixing cement and laying bricks. So Philip found himself helping to build a pigsty and, later, the coastguard hut which the boys were to man as part of their training.

Academically, Philip was not the conscientious student his son Charles was to prove himself to be. His favourite subject in schooldays, he has confessed, was 'avoiding unnecessary work'. The fact that he succeeded so well there – he shone at mathematics (which Charles didn't) as well as at geography and languages – was due to a naturally sharp, intuitive mind coupled with an upbringing which, so far, had involved three languages, English, French, German. But there was no 'avoiding unnecessary work' outside the classroom. In the open air he responded readily to Gordonstoun's character-building motto: *Plus est en vous*. He helped to man the coastguard station when it was built, a duty which boys and masters undertook in rough weather. He worked in the local smithy and went out in small boats with the local fishermen. He served as cook and lamp-trimmer for a trip to Norway on the ancient schooner the school acquired and which was later re-named *Prince Louis* in honour of his Battenberg grandfather. In the words of the school's sailing instructor, he was 'not afraid of dirty or arduous work'. He made model ships and, later, model aircraft. He played rugby football for the school, converting two tries in a game against Moray Gentlemen. He was a member of the team which Gordonstoun sent to the

Scottish schools' athletic championships in 1935 where his under-fourteen high jump of four feet five inches fell three inches short of winning. The following year, grouped with the under-sixteens, he failed to qualify in any of the three events he entered, high jump, javelin and 100 yards. But he went on eventually to captain both the cricket and hockey teams, even if hockey was a game he played with more aggression than skill. He also became a Colour Bearer and then Guardian (head boy).

He was often impatient, Hahn noted, and sometimes intolerant, facets of character he has perhaps not entirely eradicated. When he first went to Gordonstoun he was slightly boastful, claiming that one day he would be King of Greece. Only two middle-aged uncles without children stood between him and the throne, he explained. But behind the surface cockiness was a sense of insecurity which masters detected even if the other boys did not. For all his outward show of confidence he struck some of the masters as being a boy who was hungry for affection. Praise became a substitute for affection. Praise him for doing something and he would do it again, striving for improvement, eager to merit yet more praise.

Then, as later, he was far more sensitive than most people realised or he would care to admit. Just as he is easily moved to anger, so he is easily moved to laughter and, in boyhood, sometimes to tears. There was cause for tears the day Hahn broke the news to him that his sister Cecilie, her husband and their two young children had all perished in an air crash. They were bound for London to attend the wedding of Prince Louis of Hesse and the Honorable Margaret Geddes. It was foggy over Ostend and their aircraft, flying low, hit the chimney of a factory.

From time to time, during vacations, he saw his mother and sisters, and he wrote more or less regularly to his father. With one letter he enclosed a batch of fuzzy snapshots of the boys at school. He saw his father only once more. The reunion took place in Athens in 1936 when they were both there in connection with the restoration of the Greek monarchy. They discussed his future and his father suggested switching from Gordonstoun to the Greek Nautical College. Philip was not enamoured of the idea. If he was going to follow the sea, then for him, as for his Battenberg grandfather, there was only one navy – the Royal Navy. In any event, at that stage of his young life he was more inclined to favour learning to fly and going into the Royal Air Force.

From time to time, visiting London, he dropped in on his old friends, the Foufounis family, now living in a flat in Bayswater. When Hélène Foufounis (better known later as Hélène Cordet, the cabaret star) was married, her mother asked Philip to be best man. He accepted and arrived at the flat to find that both the bride and her mother had completely overlooked the question of someone to give the bride in marriage. Being Philip, he not only volunteered to fulfil both roles, best man and giver-in-marriage, but also borrowed his grandmother's car to get the bride to church on time. They were just on the point of entering the church when Hélène came to an abrupt halt. Philip, of course, knew all about last-minute nerves and how to deal with them. 'Move,' he ordered her. 'I can't,' she retorted. 'You're standing on my train.' Neither Hélène nor her husband had a job at the time. Philip, for all his youthfulness, tried to cope with that problem too. Through his grandmother he secured Hélène an introduction to the Norman Hartnell establishment. Unfortunately, they did not see her as a potential fashion model.

Philip was seventeen, fast approaching the end of his spell at Gordonstoun, when his Uncle George died and his cousin David succeeded to the title as the third Marquess of Milford Haven. With George's death, his younger brother, Louis, took over responsibility for Philip's upbringing. A more colourful and flamboyant character than his dead brother, 'Uncle Dickie', as Philip called him – the name is a diminutive of Nicholas, not the more usual Richard – quickly became the most important influence in his young life. A bond developed between them which saw Philip shattered by the brutal death of the ageing Mountbatten in 1979. To Mountbatten, Philip was like the son he had never had. Philip, for his part, found himself turning more and more to Uncle Dickie for the guidance and help not forthcoming from his absentee-father. As a teenager (and perhaps for long after) Philip completely hero-worshipped his Mountbatten uncle and modelled himself on him. And even in those early days of Mountbatten's remarkable career, before the Second World War saga of the destroyer *Kelly*, long before he became wartime head of Combined Operations and Supreme Commander in South-East Asia, there was much about Mountbatten for a young man to admire and strive to emulate. He was at that time a commander in the Royal Navy, naval ADC to King George VI, married to the immensely wealthy and attractively volatile Edwina Ashley, heiress of the Cassel millions. The pair of them lived a colourful and exciting social life and visiting them at their Park Lane home involved being whisked up in an express elevator to a luxurious two-floor apartment where Uncle Dickie's dressing room was laid out just like a cabin aboard ship. No wonder that Philip, seeking Uncle Dickie's advice as to the future, should finally forego his own preference for the Royal Air Force and follow his uncle into the Royal Navy instead.

Philip was of an age to be interested in the opposite sex. And certainly, with his blond hair and blue eyes, to arouse the interest of the opposite sex. 'Whatever you do, keep him out of girl trouble,' Philip's father wrote to Asphasia, widow of the dead King Constantine, when she invited the boy to her holiday home on a Venetian island towards the end of his time at Gordonstoun. 'He still has to pass his exams.' Prince Andrew was referring to the special entry examination Philip would have to take to qualify for the Royal Naval College, Dartmouth.

Girl trouble wasn't the only sort of trouble Asphasia had to guard against. Philip could be quite wild in those days. One night, after a drop too much to drink during a party at a taverna, he began swinging from a pergola which promptly collapsed on top of him. One particular girl took his fancy during that stay in Venice. He took her for a number of motor-boat trips and finally dated her for a moonlight cruise round the island. 'You're not to stop the engine,' Asphasia warned him. 'I shall be listening.' However, the engine stopped twice. 'Trouble with the sparking plugs,' Philip explained when he got back and waved a pair of oil-smeared hands in evidence.

It was with mixed feelings that Philip said goodbye to Gordonstoun. In many ways, he was sorry to be leaving – he had enjoyed his years there – but he was also eager to get on with the next stage of his young life. A cram course with a naval coach in Cheltenham helped him to come sixteenth out of the thirty-four would-be naval officers who took the special entrance examination. In the oral test he scored 380 marks out of a possible 400. Then, as later, he had the gift of the gab. And a confidential report from Kurt Hahn, his old headmaster at Gordonstoun, did no harm at all.

'Prince Philip is universally trusted, liked and respected,' wrote Hahn. 'He has the greatest sense of service of all the boys in the school. Prince Philip is a born leader, but will need the exacting demands of a great service to do justice to himself. His best is outstanding; his second best is not good enough. Prince Philip will make his mark in any profession where he will have to prove himself in a full trial of strength.'

Lilibet

Hélène Cordet, on the day Philip acted as both best man and giver-in-marriage at her wedding, said to him jokingly, 'How about you? When are you thinking of getting married?'

'Not for a long time,' he assured her.

Indeed, at that time he scarcely knew the girl – fourth cousin, third cousin or second cousin once removed, according to the viewpoint from which you look at their family trees – he was destined to marry. They had been briefly together upon occasion at the same royal functions, the marriage of Philip's cousin, Princess Marina, to the Duke of Kent, and the 1937 coronation of Elizabeth's father, but the difference in ages on such occasions was too great for them to have taken any real notice of each other. At the time of her father's coronation, Lilibet (as her parents called her) was only eleven, a child still; he was sixteen and already, thanks to Gordonstoun, a young man. Yet almost from the moment of her birth it was as though fate was drawing them together.

Coincidently, on the day the Queen was born, 21 April 1926, Philip's mother, Princess Alice, her sister, Louise, Crown Princess (later Queen) of Sweden, and their mother, the Dowager Marchioness of Milford Haven, were visiting Windsor Castle to have lunch with the future Queen's grandparents, King George V and Queen Mary. Coincidence, but not surprising. After all, the King and Philip's grandmother were first cousins.

Not that the marriage, when it finally came about, was an arranged one. But strong influences were to urge it forward, the Greek Royals (feeling that it would boost the shaky Greek monarchy) and the Mountbattens (who saw it as the final upward rung on their ladder of proud lineage).

Both Philip and the Queen agree that it was at Dartmouth that they first met in the sense that they walked and talked together. Not that there was anything particularly romantic about their meeting. Certainly not on Philip's side. As his romantic excursions in Venice had shown, he was of an age to be attracted to girls. But to him, that day at Dartmouth, Elizabeth seemed a child still. She was thirteen and he was eighteen, and, at those ages, the gap was impossible to bridge.

More recent writers have sometimes been scornful of the account of that first meeting given by Marion Crawford,* governess to Elizabeth and sister Margaret at the time. While conceding that hindsight may have endowed the encounter with a romantic glow it did not really have and that time may have fuzzed the edge of detail – her book was not published until eleven years after – we see no reason to doubt the general picture. She has one big advantage over other writers. She was actually there.

So what are the facts? King George VI had himself once been a cadet at Dartmouth, where he was both whacked and given an hour's drill to be carried out at the double for minor transgressions. In that last pre-war summer of 1939 he thought it would be nice to have a look at the old place again. He regarded it as a purely private visit and took his wife and two small daughters along. It was a July weekend when they arrived there aboard the old royal yacht *Victoria & Albert*. Philip's Uncle Dickie (though Marion Crawford does not mention him) was in attendance as the King's ADC. What more natural than that another royal relative, Philip, should be appointed Captain's doggie (messenger) for the day.

On the Sunday morning, 23 July 1939, there was a special service in the college chapel. Normally Elizabeth and Margaret would have attended with their parents. But because some of the college cadets had developed mumps it was felt wiser for the girls

* *The Little Princesses.*

not to go to chapel. Instead, Miss Crawford took them along to the Captain's (Sir Frederick Hew George Dalrymple-Hamilton) house to play with the Dalrymple-Hamilton children, a slightly older boy and girl. There Philip joined them presently, helping the younger children operate a toy train set, munching biscuits with them, drinking lemonade.

Marion Crawford's claim that Philip suggested going to the tennis courts and having 'some real fun' jumping the nets is perhaps open to doubt. Philip himself does not remember jumping any nets. He may have done. After all, the high jump had been one of his athletic specialities at school and schoolmates recall him leaping over the occasional tennis net in a moment of boyish exuberance. But jumping a tennis net on the spur of the moment and suggesting going out to do it as some sort of game are two very different things. The latter is something the average eighteen-year-old, and certainly one of Philip's character, would regard as childish. Particularly in view of the fact that shortly before the royal visit he had been one of the team representing Dartmouth in the Devonport Port Athletic Championship where he won the javelin event with a throw of 140 feet 10 inches.

Philip did well at Dartmouth, winning the King's Dirk for the best all-round cadet of his entry as well as the Eardley-Howard-Crockett prize, which sounds impressive but proved to be no more than a two-pound book token. Like the King before him, there was the occasional misdemeanour. He was cleared of blame the time his cutter banged into the commanding officer's boat, but another scrape resulted in his spending his eighteenth birthday digging a slit trench. As keen on sport as ever, he rowed, crewed, played squash and was a member of the second XI cricket team as well as throwing the javelin.

Most of the rest of Marion Crawford's account stands the test of critical analysis. Lunch with his royal relatives aboard the *Victoria & Albert*, both on Sunday and again the next day. Showing Lilibet and Margaret the college swimming pool. Philip himself also remembers playing croquet. Tea on the royal yacht with Philip consuming vast quantities of shrimps. He was a hearty eater in those days. And so to the final curtain.

When the royal yacht set sail again the college cadets piled into a variety of small craft to escort it out to sea. Some followed it too far, the King thought. They were signalled to turn back. All except one did so. The exception was Philip. He continued to pull lustily at the oars of the small boat he was rowing. Elizabeth (according to Miss Crawford) watched him through glasses, the King slated him as a 'young fool' and it was finally necessary to shout through a megaphone to prevail upon him to turn back.

That all this happened, or something very like it, is undoubtedly true. But that he did it to impress the thirteen-year-old Elizabeth, as some dewy-eyed writers have suggested, would seem to be nonsense. She was impressed, of course, undeniably and indelibly. But Philip did not do it for that reason. He did it, he was to say later, simply to pay his respects to his Uncle Bertie, the King.

War

The outbreak of the Second World War brought Philip a foretaste of what was to lie ahead of him in the immediate post-war
years when red tape of various sorts delayed both his naturalisation and betrothal. Not that Philip had the slightest thought of
betrothal in 1939. And Elizabeth was no more than a passing
thought the first time he sent her a Christmas card. She was
dismayed to find that his name was not on her father's list, but
finally prevailed upon him to send Philip a belated card in return.

Philip's main concern in those early days of war was to see
some action. But there were difficulties. If there was no German
taint such as that which had seen his Battenberg grandfather
hounded from his office as First Sea Lord during the First World
War, there was the fact that he was born Greek and a 'Prince of
Greece', at that, as he recorded in his midshipman's log. Greece
at the time was still neutral and if a neutral Greek prince was
killed, wounded or captured while serving on a British ship there
would undoubtedly be diplomatic repercussions. Naturalisation
would have been an easy way out, but the normal process of
naturalisation had been suspended for the duration of the war.

He took his problem to his Mountbatten mentor, Uncle
Dickie, the sort of man who could be relied upon to find a
solution. The result, in February 1940, was a posting to the
battleship *Ramillies*, based on Ceylon. It was a long way from
where the action was at the time and Philip was not exactly
thrilled. But at least he was at sea. Some of those aboard *Ramillies*
were perhaps hardly more thrilled at being landed with a Greek
prince. *Ramillies* sailed for Australia to serve as escort to troop

convoys. But the Australian troops it was escorting were destined for the Middle East, where things were beginning to hot up. That gave the naval top brass cause for further concern about Philip – they couldn't have a neutral Greek prince sculling around the Mediterranean. So Philip, after no more than a few weeks on *Ramillies*, found himself unceremoniously transferred to *Kent*, flagship of the China station. As if that wasn't safe enough for a neutral Greek, he was subsequently switched to *Lanka*, a shore station in Ceylon, and then to *Shropshire* at Durban. All this in the short space of eight months. He felt a bit like a seagoing shuttlecock.

As always, Philip had to keep busy, off duty as well as on, to question, explore, find out. During a short spell of leave while *Ramillies* was at Sydney, he hired a car and drove four hundred miles upcountry to savour the flavour of life on a sheep station. At *Lanka* he paid a similar visit to a tea plantation near Colombo, making the trip in a battered little runabout he bought for 450 rupees, half cash down, the balance paid by instalments.

The Italian invasion in October 1940 brought Greece into the war. Philip, Prince of Greece, was no longer a neutral. Now he could cheerfully be killed, wounded or taken prisoner without any bother about diplomatic repercussions. With some manoevring Philip soon managed to get himself transferred to the Mediterranean, where there was the possibility of a spot of action. He found himself aboard the battleship *Valiant* during its bombardment of Bardia and when it was attacked by enemy torpedo-bombers off Sicily.

Men who served with him at sea around this time remember him as likeable and distinctly un-royal, happy to share steaming mugs of hot cocoa with them and to accept the occasional hand-rolled cigarette. However, there seems to have been one occasion when he did pull his royal rank. Rejoining his ship late, he gave as his excuse that he had been unavoidably detained 'on business connected with the Greek Royal Family'.

With the Greeks having forced the invading Italians back into Albania, there was a spot of shore leave for Philip in Athens with cocktail parties and dances between the air raids. There was a warm reunion with his mother and he also saw something of his cousin, King George II, and other royal relatives, among them Crown Prince Paul and his wife. At one of the cocktail parties, attended by Sir Henry Channon, a small, but remarkable, incident occurred. Philip's aunt, Princess Helen, mother of Princess Marina, told Channon that her nephew was already earmarked as the future Consort of Princess Elizabeth. That was January, 1941, when Elizabeth was not yet fifteen.

If this was so, then who had done the earmarking? Not Elizabeth's father. Years later he was still to express surprise that she could have fallen in love with the first eligible young man she ever met. Princess Marina, Duchess of Kent, perhaps, Philip's cousin? Uncle Dickie? Or was it, at the time, no more than wishful thinking on Princess Helen's part? Whatever it was, her chance remark to Sir Henry Channon that night proved to be strangely prophetic.

Philip himself, today, dismisses the incident as trivial. He had no thought at the time that he might one day marry Elizabeth. No thought, indeed, of marrying anyone. There were girls, of course, in Athens, Durban and Australia, but only as casual, pleasurable companions. Nothing serious. The girl he most often escorted around at this time was his cousin, Princess Alexandra (later Queen Alexandra of Yugoslavia). She was, as she has confessed, 'a little in love with him' in those days of youth. Back in Britain there were the two daughters of Sir Harold and Lady Zia Wernher. There was a time when their mother entertained hopes that Philip might marry one of them, but Philip himself never looked on them in that light. To him they were simply nice girls to whom he was related by marriage, Lady Zia being the sister of his dead Uncle George's widow, Nadjeda.

In March 1941, at the Battle of Cape Matapan, Philip got all the action his adventurous twenty-year-old heart could desire. Britain's Mediterranean fleet, under the command of Admiral Sir Andrew Cunningham, with the light cruiser *Orion* acting as decoy to lead the Italians into ambush, trapped the Italian fleet and shattered it. It was a night engagement and Philip had charge of the searchlights on the engaged side.

One writer has given an almost *Boys' Own* paper account of the action in which the youthful Philip operated his searchlights while cannon shells from enemy bombers 'ripped down the pathways of golden beams'. It wasn't quite like that, though hardly less dramatic. The searchlight beams were horizontal, not vertical, lighting up enemy ships, not bombers. Even as Philip brought his lights to bear on the Italian cruiser *Fiume*, a broadside from the flagship *Warspite* tore into it. *Valiant*'s own broadside followed seconds later. With *Fiume* wrecked and burning, there were shouts from *Valiant*'s bridge for the searchlights to bear left. Philip operated them accordingly and picked up another Italian cruiser *Zara*. Five more broadsides left that shattered and sinking too. By the time it was all over the Italians had lost four cruisers and two destroyers; had another destroyer and a brand-new battleship severely damaged. For his part in the action Philip was mentioned in despatches: 'Thanks to his alertness and appreciation of the situation we were able to sink in five minutes two eight-inch gun cruisers.' His native Greece did him rather better. They gave him the War Cross.

The dancing and cocktail parties in Athens came to an abrupt halt as the Germans threw their weight alongside the Italians and began to overrun the country. Most of the Greek Royals took temporary refuge on Crete and then when Crete, too, came under attack, were evacuated from there to Alexandria by destroyer and flying boat. But not Philip's mother. British by birth, married to an exiled Greek prince, her three surviving daughters married to Germans while her son was serving in the Royal Navy, she saw her own duty with crystal clarity. It was to her adopted homeland of Greece. So she stayed on in Athens, doing hospital work, taking a small group of war orphans under her wing and, on one occasion at least, loftily defying the German invaders. Always an intensely religious woman, her experiences in wartime Greece made her increasingly so. She sold much of her personal jewellery to raise funds for Greek relief and, after the war, retreated to the island of Tinos where she founded her own religious order. Later she again returned to Athens where she ran the Order of Martha and Mary as a training school for nurses. But it didn't work out and at the age of 75, reluctantly, she was forced to close it down.

Valiant, with Philip aboard, was involved in the battle for Crete – until an enemy bomb amidships caused it to limp away to Alexandria for repairs. For Philip, there was a brief reunion with his cousin David, also serving in the Royal Navy at the time, and with Uncle Dickie, more a hero to him than ever after being snatched from the sea, along with only 109 other survivors out of a ship's complement of 240, when his destroyer *Kelly* was sunk.

About the time of his twentieth birthday in the summer of 1941 Philip was ordered back to Britain to take his sub-lieutenant's examination. But getting there, in those days of war, was something easier said than done. With the Mediterranean now dominated by German aircraft, it involved a lengthy round-about trip, starting aboard a troopship bound for Durban. There was some delay in Durban before he could transfer to another ship and he linked up with another of his many royal relatives, Crown Princess Frederika. She had a car, which saved him the expense of hiring one, and he used it to explore Cape Province. There was also some enjoyable late-night shore leave in pleasurable feminine company even if the pleasures of the night were too often tarnished by the necessity to be up early for field training the following morning. He also took advantage of the delay to catch up on his letter writing. One of the letters he wrote was to Elizabeth, in answer to one received from her. Elizabeth, in those wartime days, was a great letter-writer, forever sending letters of encouragement and good cheer, written in a scrawling schoolgirl hand, to relatives and royal servants in the armed forces.

The only way for Philip to get back to Britain, it seemed, was to go first to Canada. Along with a bunch of other young midshipmen, he boarded a troopship, bound for Halifax. At Puerto Rico the Chinese stokers in the boiler room decided to abandon ship and Philip and his companions found themselves heaving coal in their place. It is said that he volunteered for the job, which is not unlikely, and at the end of the voyage he merited a certificate proclaiming him to be 'a qualified coal trimmer'. He also ended the voyage with hands so blistered that he had some

[48]

difficulty manipulating his knife and fork and had to resort to eating American-style for a time. When the ship berthed at Newport News, Virginia, before going on to Halifax, he did his usual trick of renting a car and exploring the area. He drove as far as Washington and back.

Eventually he made it back to Britain where he successfully passed the examination which had involved so long a journey and was promoted to sub-lieutenant on 1 February 1942. There was some leave due to him and he spent it with his grandmother at Kensington Palace. He also visited Royal Lodge, Windsor, to see the King and Queen. They invited him to stay for tea, for which Margaret and Elizabeth joined them.

There was also an invitation to Coppins, the country home of the Kents. His cousin, Princess Marina, whose husband was to be killed soon after in a wartime air crash, invited him to a dance to celebrate her wedding anniversary. Perhaps she was trying her hand at a spot of match-making by inviting Elizabeth also, now in her mid-teens. The two of them danced together for the first time.

Romantically, Philip was still footloose and fancy free. On leave, he was constantly pursued by girls – they wrote; they telephoned – and he probably rather enjoyed their adulation, as would most young men. Whether or not he was actually saving himself for Elizabeth, he appears to have given some girls a rather hard time. One he dated telephoned his grandmother's Kensington Palace home in anticipation of a further date only to be informed that he had gone away. He had – but not all that far. He had moved into Uncle Dickie's wartime home in Chester Street.

While in London on leave he ran into his childhood friend, Hélène Foufounis as was. He went to see a Disney movie with her and her husband and then on to dinner at a club of which the husband was a member. Not being a member himself, Philip had to sign in. He signed the register simply 'Philip'.

'I'm afraid we require your surname, sir', said the receptionist.

So Philip added 'of Greece'.

[49]

The receptionist thought he was trying to take the mickey. 'A joke is a joke, sir, but we still need your full name.'

It was Hélène who explained that he was Prince Philip.

It was not the first time that Philip had come up against this embarrassing problem of signatures . . . and it would not be the last.

As sub-lieutenant, Philip was posted to *Wallace*, a destroyer engaged on convoy duty in the Channel and the North Sea. Nine months later he was promoted to the rank of lieutenant and appointed second in command. Promotion was normal; the appointment was at his captain's request. Second in command of another destroyer in the same squadron, *Lauderdale*, was a breezy young Australian, Michael Parker. He and Philip turned out to be two of a kind, hard-working and conscientious on duty, high-spirited and skylarking when not. It became something of a point of honour between them as to which ran the tightest ship. Shipboard rivalry developed into a close and rollicking friendship which was later to result in Philip, feeling the need of moral support in his new and much more public role of royal son-in-law, seeking Parker's support.

Among Philip's Christmas cards that year was one from Elizabeth, enclosing a photograph of herself. He decided to send her one in return. But the only photo to hand was one in the rank of sub-lieutenant which had been taken prior to his latest promotion. So he sent that and for some time it occupied pride of place on her mantelpiece until it was replaced by a photograph showing a bearded and less easily recognisable Philip. Today both photographs, bearded and clean-shaven, are among the collection of family photos which clutter the Queen's desk.

The *Wallace*, with Philip aboard, provided cover for the Canadian landing in Sicily and it was perhaps around this time also that it was berthed alongside a Canadian destroyer at Scapa Flow. Philip harked back to the occasion years later when addressing a reunion dinner of Canadian war correspondents. 'It didn't last long,' he recalled, 'which may have been a good thing because we soon lost track of where one hangover ended and the next began.'

He spent part of one leave with the Royal Family at Windsor. Always a good talker, he amused the King and Queen with his jaunty tales of shipboard life. Both enjoyed his sense of humour. More seriously, he also told the King something of the grimmer side of the war at sea. Matapan, he said, was 'as near murder as anything can be in wartime. We just smashed the Italian cruisers. They burst into tremendous sheets of flame.'

With *Wallace* back in Britain for a refit after the Sicily landing, he was again invited to Windsor around Christmas. His cousin, David Milford-Haven, was invited too. They sat with the King and Queen in the Waterloo Room to watch one of the amateur pantomimes regularly staged at Windsor over Christmas. The valuable oil paintings which normally fill the walls of the Waterloo Room had been removed from their frames for safe keeping. In their place, in line with the temporary theatrical atmosphere, were colourful illustrations of various pantomime characters, Mother Goose, Dick Whittington and the like. 'My ancestors,' the King joked.

That year's pantomime was *Aladdin and His Wonderful Lamp* and Philip was given a programme with an appropriate willow-pattern design on the cover. A lot of jokes about 'the Castle' and other royal topics had been dovetailed into the traditional script. Margaret had the part of Roxane while Elizabeth, in a short tunic and silk tights, played the title role of Aladdin. She was not quite eighteen.

Whether or not Princess Marina had been match-making when she invited Elizabeth and Philip to that anniversary dance at Coppins, others were now quite convinced that the two of them should marry. And soon. When Philip's cousin, Alexandra, who had earlier fancied herself 'a little in love with him', married King Peter of Yugoslavia at the Yugoslav Embassy in London, in March 1944, it was King George II of Greece, another cousin, who gave her in marriage while King George VI of Britain served as Peter's best man. The scent of orange blossom being in the air, George II seized the opportunity to broach the question of Philip marrying George VI's daughter.

Elizabeth's father was taken aback. He knew that his daughter was forever talking about Philip, but he had no idea that things had reached this sort of stage. Whatever was being whispered and hatched among the Greek Royals, he had no intention that Elizabeth should marry anyone yet awhile. He hastened to assure the Greek king that he liked young Philip. 'He is intelligent, has a good sense of humour and thinks about things the right way.' On, no, he had nothing against Philip, but Elizabeth was too young for any talk of marriage.

How far Philip himself was aware of this special spot of pleading on his behalf it is impossible to say, but that his feelings for Elizabeth were developing into something more than mere friendship was revealed in Australia not long after. Philip had made friends with a couple named Joe and Judy Fallon. One day Judy caught him looking at a newspaper photograph of the royal sisters, Elizabeth and Margaret. 'You've picked the wrong one,' she joked. 'Margaret's the better-looking.'

As a joke it misfired rather badly. Philip looked furious instead of amused. He screwed up the newspaper and threw it across the room. 'You wouldn't say that if you knew them,' he snapped. 'Elizabeth is sweet and kind — just like her mother.'

Philip had been transferred from *Wallace* to *Whelp*, a new destroyer awaiting commissioning. At Newcastle upon Tyne, while waiting for the ship, he stayed in a modestly small hotel, travelling to and from the shipyard each day by bus. His keen rival and firm friend, Mike Parker, was transferred to the destroyer *Wessex* at the same time. Both ships were part of the 27th Destroyer Flotilla and together they sailed for the Far East to do battle with the Japanese off Burma and Sumatra. There was a spot of shore leave in Australia where the old business of his signature cropped up yet again. Hiring a car for one of his exploration sorties, he signed the rental form 'Philip' as usual. If a London receptionist could made so much fuss over a name, you can guess what sort of reception he got from a hard-bitten Australian car-hire man.

If Philip and Parker had shore leave at the same time, then the fun was fast and furious. There was a day at the races when the crowd got wind of Philip's presence and clamoured to know which was the prince. Parker was sporting a beard at the time; Philip had just shaved his off. 'The one with the beard,' lied Philip, to Parker's considerable embarrassment.

They were accompanied on that day at the races by some attractive girls, among them Parker's sister. There were other girls on other occasions, though Philip was now increasingly careful never to get too involved. There was one night, at the end of a dance, when he found himself landed with a particularly pretty girl. The problem was what to do with her. He could hardly walk off and leave her to her own devices. That would be impolite. On the other hand, to see her home might spark off just the sort of gossip he was most anxious to avoid. He solved the problem by taking her round to the Fallons, where he flopped out in a chair and apparently dozed off. Time passed, the girl became fidgety and finally Joe Fallon took her home. No sooner had the door closed behind them than Philip opened his eyes and gave a broad grin. Problem solved, situation under control.

On 2 September 1945 Philip was privileged to be aboard Admiral William Halsey's USS *Missouri* to witness Japan's formal and unconditional surrender. It was not until early the following year that he arrived back in Britain, bringing with him a shipload of freed POWs.

Courtship

Philip was almost twenty-five when he returned to Britain at the end of the war. Time to give serious thought to the future. He discussed the idea of a naval career with Uncle Dickie, who was all for it. To obtain a permanent commission, however, meant becoming a British citizen and naturalisation procedures were still in a state of wartime suspension. Moreover, Philip was more than merely Greek by birth. He was also a Prince of Greece. He therefore discussed the situation with his cousin, King George II. Perhaps more in the hope of a matrimonial alliance with Britain than with the idea of furthering Philip's naval career, Cousin George raised no objection to the idea that he should discard his title and renounce his right of succession to the Greek throne.

Whelp was transferred to the reserve and Philip was given charge of the de-commissioning process. That done, he was transferred to HMS *Glendower*, a shore establishment in Wales. An obliging – and surprised – night porter at a local hotel found himself being given letters to post addressed to 'Her Royal Highness The Princess Elizabeth'.

Philip had not seen his father since he was a schoolboy at Gordonstoun. There was no possibility now that he would ever see him again. Prince Andrew had died of a heart attack in Monte Carlo towards the end of 1944 at the age of sixty-two. Philip attended a memorial service to him and set about the job of winding up his estate. It was not a very onerous business. Even in those days a tax-free annuity of £750 a year, which Andrew had obtained from his nephew, King George II, in exchange for the villa on Corfu, did not go far in a place like Monte Carlo. About all that Philip was left with when everything was settled was his father's signet ring, a shaving brush which he had refurbished with new bristles and some suits which he had altered to fit him. He was still wearing one of the suits from time to time six years later.

Family affairs of a more pleasurable nature required him to go to Lake Constance. He has always been close to the youngest of his sisters, Sophie (though he calls her 'Tiny'), perhaps because she was the nearest to his own age, and the occasion was her second marriage. Her first husband, Christopher of Hesse, had been killed during the war, while flying with the Luftwaffe in Italy. Now she became Princess George of Hanover.

He visited Paris where he ran into Hélène Cordet née Foufounis again. He was, she discovered, still the same old Philip, inviting her to tea at the Ritz and then turning up on a ladies' bicycle much too small for his lanky frame which he pedalled furiously, knees almost touching his chin, along the Champs Elysées. Another evening he took her for coffee at the Trocadero. They drove there in a fiacre. Philip thought it highly amusing that they should be travelling in so romantic a conveyance 'and we're just two old childhood friends'.

From *Glendower* Philip was transferred to HMS *Royal Arthur*, another shore establishment and a lot less fancy than its name might suggest. It was no more than a cluster of huts near Corsham in Wiltshire. His job was to lecture petty officers on naval warfare and current affairs, and one who was there at the time remembers Philip as enjoying nothing so much as a good argument. As in childhood, life for Philip at this time was a curious mixture of the grand and the commonplace. There were, on the one hand, secretive telephone calls to the King's daughter at Buckingham Palace and, on the other, pints of beer and games of skittles in the local pub, the *Methuen Arms*.

He bought an MG sports car to facilitate getting backwards and forwards to London. His destination was sometimes Buckingham Palace, but more often the Royal Lodge at Windsor, where the King liked to relax at weekends. Of course Philip did not go primarily to see the King, but his elder daughter. His courtship of her adhered to the accepted pattern of a quieter, less permissive age. They walked the corgis together and went riding in Windsor Great Park. They played croquet on the lawn and sometimes, if the weather was warm enough, swam in the blue-tiled pool. They were seldom alone. Usually Elizabeth's parents were around. Or servants. Even if they went out for a walk they would find a giggling teenage chatterbox named Margaret tagging along. To avoid gossip, and speculative newspaper head-lines, public outings had to be circumspect. So theatre visits meant a party of six or eight. It was as two of a party that they went to the theatre on Elizabeth's twentieth birthday. Looking back, it seems oddly prophetic that the play they saw that evening was titled *The First Gentleman*, a title Philip was subse-quently to be accorded as Elizabeth's husband.

About the only opportunity they had of being alone together was when Philip took Elizabeth for a spin in the MG. Accus-tomed to rather grander cars in her role as royal princess, she felt as though she was 'sitting on the ground', she said. Sometimes they drove over to Coppins where Philip's cousin, Marina, Duchess of Kent, was always romantically eager to give court-ship a helping hand.

When Elizabeth and Margaret returned to Buckingham Palace from Royal Lodge on Sunday evenings, Philip sometimes went too. But not with the two princesses. Someone might spot him and speculation might start. So he drove on ahead in the MG while they followed at more leisurely pace in a more stately car. If Philip stayed in London overnight, it would be at his grand-mother's apartment in Kensington Palace or at Uncle Dickie's home in Chester Street where a camp bed was no more uncom-fortable than a naval bunk. At the palace, he was careful to avoid the ever-present sightseers at the main gate and drive in surrep-titiously by a side entrance. A former palace servant remembers seeing Philip tinkering with the innards of his car in the inner quadrangle on one occasion while Elizabeth looked on with interest. The wonder was that she did not pitch in and help. After all, it was not long since she had taken a vehicle maintenance course as a second subaltern in the ATS. So she knew all about adjusting carburettors, grinding valves and decarbonising cylinder heads. Probably, like a sensible girl, she managed to keep her mouth shut while he did things all wrong.

If Philip was careful not to stir up gossip and specualtion about the two of them, some of his Greek relatives, perhaps for their own reasons, were rather less cautious. A leak from one of them, accidental or otherwise, saw the first engagement rumour headlined in an Athens newspaper. It was promptly denied from Buckingham Palace. There were to be other newspaper stories of imminent engagement over the next twelve months. And always a quick official denial. The denials made prior to the visit Philip paid to Balmoral, in Scotland, that summer were undeniably true. But those issued afterwards were true only inasmuch as Elizabeth's father had still to sanction an official betrothal. As far as Philip and Elizabeth were concerned, after that visit to Scotland they were already betrothed.

King George VI, though he had been told about Elizabeth and Philip by Greece's George II, still found it almost impossible to believe that his elder daughter had fallen in love with just about the first eligible young man she had ever met. He thought she should look around a bit more before jumping into marriage. As a King's daughter does not have much opportunity to look around on her own account, her father did it for her, inviting a succession of eligible young men, the heirs to dukedoms and earldoms, to Sandringham at Christmas, to Windsor for Ascot week and to Balmoral ahead of Philip. Those who guessed why they had been invited also knew that they stood very little chance and, after Philip's stay at Balmoral, no chance at all, though royal servants at one stage, indulging in backstairs gossip, were inclined to bet on Lord Porchester rather than Philip as the future Consort. But he became her racing manager instead.

Philip arrived at Balmoral with the rather slender wardrobe of most young officers who had gone almost straight from school into the war-time navy; 'one of the generation,' he has said, 'who started the war in nappies, spent the next few years in uniform and when peace broke out, found myself without any other clothes.' He took no pyjamas with him (you did not bother with such niceties in the navy) and no slippers. He did take some spare shirts and socks. Also a dinner jacket obligingly loaned to him by Uncle Dickie as they took the same size. He was later reported to have gone grouse-shooting with the King in 'well-fitting sports clothes'. Well-fitting they may have been, but his 'sports clothes' consisted of flannels and sweater, though he was to acquire a pair of knickerbockers for subsequent royal shooting expeditions. The shoes he wore on the moors proved insufficiently robust to endure the onslaughts of Scottish heather and had to be sent over to a cobbler in nearby Crathie for emergency repairs. Then, as now, the atmosphere at Balmoral was heavy with tartan and the glassy-eyed heads of long dead stags. He was given one of the ground-floor guest rooms, all brass and marble and darkly solid Victorian furniture. Hot water for shaving was brought to him each morning in a brass jug with a towel draped over it to keep the heat in.

Where and how the Queen and Philip reached their final romantic understanding is, like the inscription engraved inside the Queen's wedding ring, their personal secret. Which is as it should be. But there could be no official announcement as yet. There were many problems and difficulties to be smoothed out first. One of the problems was the question of Philip's naturalisation. His cousin, the Greek king, who had earlier been all in favour of naturalisation and marriage, was now worried that for a Greek prince to suddenly become a naturalised Briton might tilt the scales against the restoration of monarchy in Greece. Philip called on his Greek cousin in his suite at Claridges in an attempt to iron things out, but to no avail. He sought the help of Uncle Dickie who wrote to King George VI in an effort to hurry things along.

Elizabeth's father was himself in no hurry to see his elder daughter married. Not that he had anything against Philip. The more he came to know him, the more he liked him. The two of them spoke the same blunt navy-type language and had the same banana-skin sense of humour. But the King was also possessive of the daughter who would one day succeed him on the throne and, like many fathers, was inclined to resent the idea of surrendering her to another and younger man. But he was also a sensitive man who was later to feel, as he said in a letter, that he had perhaps been a little hard-hearted in making them wait so long.

Back from Balmoral, the young couple occasionally went night-clubbing or to the theatre together, though never as a twosome, but always in a party of four or more in the unrealised hope that this would arouse less gossip and speculation. One of their theatre outings was to the American musical *Oklahoma!* when it opened in London. One of the hit tunes from the show, 'People Will Say We're In Love', became 'their tune' for a time and, in the privacy of her palace apartment, Elizabeth played a recording of it over and over again until it was almost worn out.

Philip spent his Christmas leave at Sandringham with the Royals and again went out shooting with the King, mainly pheasants and partridges at Sandringham as against grouse at Balmoral. He was, at the time, neither a particularly good shot nor especially enamoured of the sport. But the King – one of the best shots in the country – was addicted to it and anything which might commend Philip to his prospective father-in-law was to be persevered with. So Philip sought advice on improving his marksmanship. 'If you can hit woodcock, you can hit anything,' he was told. Solo expeditions in pursuit of woodcock, therefore became the order of the day and in time Philip, in turn, was to rank among the best shots in Britain, though not so good, royal gamekeepers have been heard to say, as his son, Charles.

The fact that he was at Sandringham and had previously been at Balmoral did not escape the notice of the newspapers, of course. Headlines againt hinted at pending betrothal and one newspaper asked its readers to vote on the question: Is Philip The Right Man For The Princess? Fifty-five per cent said Yes, forty per cent said No and five per cent didn't know. The main objection of those who voted 'No' was on the basis of nationality. He wasn't British, was he? Greek or something, wasn't he? There was a lot of uncertainty. But some people knew that his sisters were married to Germans and liked that idea even less.

Nor were the newspaper voters the only ones who were troubled about such things. A plebiscite in Greece favoured the return of the monarchy and George II went back to Athens as King. But he still felt that for Philip to become a naturalised Briton might tilt the delicate balance in a county teetering on the verge of civil war. In Britain, the Cabinet, informed by King George VI of his daughter's wish to marry Philip, was hardly enthusiastic even if it raised no formal objection to the match. As with the newspaper readers, some didn't like his German connections while others were not happy about him having been born a Prince of Greece. Ernest Bevin, the Foreign Secretary, was especially doubtful about announcing a betrothal while British troops remained in Greece bolstering the recently restored monarchy.

Philip became increasingly impatient and irritated with all the delay. Rightly or wrongly, he blamed the newspapers, their gossip and speculation, for some of the difficulties he experienced at this time. If the cause is forgotten all these years later, some of the effect remains and the resentment of the press which he sometimes displays dates from that time. Elizabeth, too, was unhappy over the delay and Margaret sensed her sister's unease. 'His not being English, does it make a difference?' she asked her governess, Marion Crawford.

To keep things in as low a key as possible, it was deemed advisable for Philip's naturalisation to be processed while the Royal Family was away touring South Africa. The question arose as to what he should be called when he became a British citizen. His future father-in-law thought it would be a good idea if His Royal Highness was substituted for Prince of Greece. Uncle Dickie liked the idea, too, and prime minister Clement Attlee, when the matter was raised with him, had no objection. The one who objected was Philip. For the time being, at least, he had had quite enough of signing 'Philip' only to be asked by club receptionists and car hire dealers, 'Philip who?'

But if he wasn't to have a title, he needed a name. His family name of Schleswig-Holstein-Sonderburg-Glücksburg was too much for ordinary consumption. The College of Heralds was called in to advise and suggested Philip Oldcastle, the name

[60]

being an anglicized version of Oldenburg which was also some-where in his complex lineage. Then Chuter Ede, the Home Secretary, suggested the anglicised version of Battenberg with which the public was already familiar – Mountbatten. No prizes for guessing how Chuter Ede got that idea. Philip's Uncle Dickie, now Earl Mountbatten of Burma, had finally yielded to the Government's request and accepted the thankless task of becoming the last Viceroy of India. Philip himself, initially, was not especially enthused. Fond as he was of Mountbatten, he did not want to live in the great man's shadow. But in the absence of any other worthwhile suggestion, he agreed.

As one of his last acts before leaving for India, Mountbatten slyly invited the chairman of the Beaverbrook newspaper group, together with the editors of its daily and Sunday newspapers, round for drinks. If there was to be opposition to the betrothal announcement when it came, the Beaverbrook press, not exactly noted for its admiration of the Mountbatten clan, would be in the van. Almost casually, or so it seemed at the time, he introduced the fair-haired young man who handed round the drinks as his nephew, Philip. He needed some advice, he said, on what the public reaction was likely to be to the idea of Philip becoming British. No mention of any betrothal, naturally. Advice was readily forthcoming and Mountbatten expressed his gratitude, congratulating himself that he had effectively cut off the legs of the opposition.

It was natural that Elizabeth should have wanted Philip to see her off when the Royals sailed for South Africa on the battleship *Vanguard*. Her father shook his head. Betrothal rumours having been several times denied, it wouldn't do at all, he said. But he saw no harm in a small private dinner party at the Mountbatten residence a night or two before they sailed. It was, to all intents and purposes, an unofficial betrothal party even if any official announcement must still wait upon events.

Philip's naturalisation was processed while the Royals were out of the country. He submitted his application through his commanding officer who was required to certify that he was of good character, had assimilated the British way of life and would make a good citizen. Philip himself stated on the application form that he had an adequate knowledge of the English language, was financially solvent and would either continue in the armed forces or take up residence in one of what were then 'the Dominions'. He was listed as Mountbatten, Philip, born in Greece. His occupation was given as a serving officer in His Majesty's Forces and his address as 16 Chester Street, London SW1, the Mountbatten residence. The whole business cost him £10 plus a further half-crown (13p) for the Commissioner of Oaths before whom he took the oath of allegiance.

With the Royal Family's return from South Africa, Lieutenant Philip Mountbatten, as he now was, became a more frequent visitor to Buckingham Palace, even if he was still fairly circumspect about his comings and goings. Almost a member of the family already, he joined a luncheon party held to celebrate the eightieth birthday of Elizabeth's grandmother, Queen Mary. The court circular during Royal Ascot week made no mention of his presence, but he was there just the same, at least for the last-night dance in Windsor Castle which wound up the week's enjoyment. His mother arrived in England and moved in with her mother at Kensington Palace. Philip took Elizabeth there to see her. It was the first time mother and bride-to-be had met.

For one old shipmate to call on another, the day Michael Parker visited Corsham, seemed natural enough and attracted no publicity. In fact, the meeting was a lot less casual than it seemed. Parker was now married – he met his wife, Eileen, while she was serving in the WRNS – and invalided out of the Navy. His father-in-law had obligingly found him a job in the London office of the family rope-making concern. It proved to be rather too tame a life for the rumbustious Parker and he was toying with the idea of packing it in and returning to Australia when Philip sent word that he would like to see him. Nervous of the new life he knew would lie ahead of him once he was married to the Princess and feeling in need of moral support, Philip let Parker into the secret of what was in the wind and offered him a job. Not as his private secretary, the role for which Parker is mainly remembered. That did not come until later, when the Princess became the Queen and Philip became her Consort. Before that he did not merit a private secretary and the bride-to-be already had one. So the job he offered Parker initially was as equerry to them both. Parker jumped at it.

On 8 July Philip drove yet again to Buckingham Palace. But this time he took a suitcase with him. Also the engagement ring he had had made. The diamonds in it had been taken from another ring his father had given his mother years before and which she had now given him in turn. Because of the need for secrecy, not even the jeweller who fashioned the ring knew who it was for. There had thus been no opportunity for Elizabeth to try it on. When Philip finally slipped it on her finger it proved to be fractionally too large and had to be altered later.

He was given the ground floor Buhl Room at the palace, in which his son, Charles, was later to be born. Elizabeth did not like his smoking and he had promised to give it up. But he lit up on that first night at Buckingham Palace. Nerves, perhaps. In fact, he continued to smoke intermittently during the four months of their engagement, but gave it up completely once he was married. Looking out of the window of the Buhl Room, he decided that the Victoria Memorial, just across from the palace gates, offered a too tempting vantage point for some sufficiently enterprising photographer. 'Draw the curtains,' he instructed the palace footman detailed to valet him.

He had no valet of his own – until now there had been no need of one – and was later to take over Uncle Dickie's butler, John Dean, as valet. Indeed, at this time he still had few clothes, at least by the standards of royal life. That deficiency was quickly remedied. A tailor was summoned next day to measure him for some new suits. Extra shirts, shoes from Lobb and a topper from Lock's followed in rapid succession.

While Philip was being measured for new suits the following day, Elizabeth attended the International Horse Show in company with her parents. The backstairs quarters of the palace were alive with gossip. 'What's he like?' everyone wanted to know. For all Philip's comings and goings, few of the palace staff had seen him. 'Absolutely dishy,' said a maid who had dusted his room and nearly swooned when she found herself almost face to face with him.

That evening the betrothal became official. Philip gave Elizabeth the engagement ring and she wore it when they joined her parents for a small celebration dinner. In Fleet Street and at Broadcasting House editors and newscasters fidgeted over the official announcement which they were embargoed from making public until half-past midnight. With the expiration of the embargo, the betrothal, so often rumoured and so often denied, was finally a reality:

'It is with great pleasure that the King and Queen announce the betrothal of their dearly-beloved daughter The Princess Elizabeth to Lieutenant Philip Mountbatten, RN, son of the late Prince Andrew of Greece and Princess Andrew (Princess Alice of Battenberg), to which union the King has gladly given his consent.'

Public Property

With the official admission that he was betrothed to the King's daughter, Philip's life underwent a sudden and drastic change. Until then, he had always been his own man, speaking his mind, doing his own thing. All at once he was everybody's man, public property. The fact that he was marrying into the Royal Family meant, as another free spirit, the Queen Mother, had realised years before (giving her cause for the briefest of hesitations before entering into her own marriage), that from now on he was no longer free to do what he wanted, say what he liked, hardly to think his own thoughts. It is not in Philip's nature to efface himself to quite that extent and the time was to come when he would break the rules. And pay the penalty.

The strictures of his new royal role were not too apparent at the outset and he took most of what came his way in good part, making a smiling first appearance on Buckingham Palace's famous balcony with his bride-to-be and posing happily with her for the benefit of photographers. There was no thought in his mind that the time would come when he would find the persistent attention of photographers a lot less welcome.

He was delighted when the London Federation of Boys' Clubs, quick to get in on the new royal act, asked him to become its patron. He can hardly have envisaged the scores of similar requests with which he would be bombarded over the next thirty years or so. It was with some degree of pride that he revisited his old school to deliver his maiden speech at Cheam's tercentenary celebrations. If he had any thought of the dozens of speeches he would be required to make in the future – so many that it would

5 [65]

require an index system to avoid repeating himself – it was probably with a grin of delight. He went back to Corsham to open a garden of remembrance there to the village's wartime dead – the start of a production line of openings, unveilings, inspections, tree plantings, launchings, luncheons, banquets, handshakes, with which he would have to contend non-stop from then on.

It was, in the beginning, all something of a novelty and he found it fun. He was the new blue-eyed boy of the Royal Family and could do no wrong. There was not a hint of criticism and he cannot possibly have foreseen all the digs, snipes, sneers, attacks which would come later. But his father-in-law did. 'It's a good job Philip's got broad shoulders,' he remarked, prophetically.

The magic was perhaps already beginning to rub a little thin even before the marriage, as witness the day Philip stalked over to one of the photographers tailing him and Elizabeth. 'Congratulations,' he said. The photographer, looking understandably puzzled, asked what the congratulations were for. 'Because you're the only one who stands up straight and takes your picture without a lot of contortions,' Philip informed him.

That was on the Isle of Arran which he visited in the company of Elizabeth and her parents. Perhaps there was also a glimpse that day of the new touch Philip would bring to bear on the ancient institution of Monarchy. The King and Queen were in one car for a two-hour tour of the island; Philip and Elizabeth in another. However, while the King and Queen were chauffeur-driven, Philip did the driving in the other car with Elizabeth beside him and their chauffeur and the accompanying detective in the back. If the King was somewhat surprised by this change, he offered no objection other than to murmur 'It's a very heavy car.'

There were visits to Edinburgh and elsewhere so that the King's subjects could see what they – and Elizabeth – were getting. In Edinburgh Elizabeth was given the Freedom of the City. Philip himself was later to be given the Freedom of the same city and came to tell a rollicking tale about the occasion in later years.... 'We were just about to leave again when someone said

[66]

the train was twenty minutes late. The Lord Provost rushed round and refilled the glasses. As we were finishing, someone else said the train was still twenty minutes late. This continued for some time and eventually we decided that the train was six drinks late. When we came out of the hotel many citizens must have marvelled to see their Lord Provost and myself on such exceeding good terms.'

On that first visit to Edinburgh, at a ball in the Assembly Rooms, Philip found himself relegated to the sidelines, looking on while someone else partnered Elizabeth in the opening dance, a double eightsome reel. As with shooting at Sandringham, so with Scottish dancing in Edinburgh – he had Elizabeth and the King's piper give him a crash course in the subject and picked it up quickly enough to partner Elizabeth himself at a second ball a couple of nights later.

There was an early brush with the press when his car skidded into a tree on the way back to Corsham and he was compelled to thumb a lift from a passing motorist. The following day found the newspapers wagging reproving editorial fingers. In fact, Philip had got in first. Realising that the story of his mishap was bound to make the headlines, he had put through a call to Buckingham Palace immediately he got back to Corsham to give Elizabeth his own account of what had happened.

He was not yet as allergic to some sections of the press as he was to become later. However, growing antipathy was hardly eased when he heard from Paris that a magazine had been trying to buy a photograph of himself and Hélène Cordet from her brother, Ianni Foufounis. The photograph was innocent enough, taken years before when he had filled the double role of best man and giver-in-marriage at her wedding. It is doubtful if the magazine, had it succeeded in obtaining the photograph, would have captioned it as such.

Even more than most bridegrooms, he found himself forced to take a back seat in the arrangements for his own wedding. When the bride is a future Queen, even the bride's mother does not have all that much of a say. The wedding becomes a national event and other forces move in and take over. Even the one thing

[67]

all other bridegrooms do – provide their own wedding ring – was barred to Philip. Elizabeth's wedding ring was fashioned from a chunk of Welsh gold presented by the people of Wales.

From all parts of the world wedding gifts poured in. If most gifts were slanted towards the bride or intended to help the newlyweds furnish their future home; Philip did not come out of it too badly. There were, among other gifts, two sailboats, *Coweslip* and *Bluebottle*, a brace of Purdey guns from his father-in-law, a walking stick from the Moonrakers, the skittles team of which he had been a member at the *Methuen Arms*, and a duffel coat from an American living in the beer-brewing city of Milwaukee.

The hardest blow of all for him to bear in the preparations for the wedding was the fact that his sisters' names were not included on the invitation list. Invitations could go to his mother and other relatives, even to old friends like Hélène Cordet and her mother, Anna Foufounis, but not to his sisters. By marrying Germans they had become German nationals and the memory of the Second World War was still too fresh in British minds for anyone German, however closely related, to be invited. The best Philip could do was arrange for an extra set of wedding photographs to be printed for his sisters. His cousin, Princess Marina, obligingly flew out to Germany with them shortly after the wedding.

From all directions fingers were poked in the pie of the royal marriage. The Archbishop of Canterbury, Dr Fisher, was not happy with the idea that Philip had been baptised into the Greek Orthodox Church even though he had worshipped as an Anglican during his years in the Navy. Being a Greek Orthodox was not as bad as being a Catholic, of course, but better if the boy was Church of England. So a quiet ceremony to effect the transfer of religious allegiance was arranged in the chapel at Lambeth Palace. Philip is said to have quipped that not everyone gets married within a couple of months of being baptised.

His future place in the royal pecking order was emphasised by the King's award of the Order of the Garter to both him and Elizabeth. Philip got his eight days after it had been bestowed upon the bride-to-be. Nor, for all that he was listed as plain Lieutenant Philip Mountbatten, RN, in the order of service for the wedding ceremony (because it had been printed some time ahead), was it a humble naval lieutenant who was married in Westminster Abbey on 20 November 1947. To King George VI, it was unthinkable that his elder daughter, the future Queen, should emerge from the Abbey as Princess Mrs Lieutenant Mountbatten. So, with only twenty-four hours to go, he elevated his future son-in-law to the triple title of Duke of Edinburgh, Earl of Merioneth and Baron Greenwich. 'It is a great deal to give a man all at once,' the King noted, 'but I know Philip understands his responsibilities on his marriage to Lilibet.'

The King did not, however, give back to Philip the title of Prince which he had relinquished in order to become a naturalised British citizen. This was not a deliberate omission on George VI's part but due to his misunderstanding of the situation. The King thought that, by giving Philip the style of His Royal Highness, he was automatically making him a Prince. In fact, he was not, and it was not until several years after succeeding to the throne that Elizabeth put right what her father had inadvertently done wrong. However, niceties of this sort were completely lost on the British public to whom the Consort has consistently been known as Prince Philip.

He was married from his grandmother's apartment at Kensington Palace. The night before the wedding there was the traditional stag party to mark the end of his bachelor status. In fact, there were two. The first was an enjoyable, but hardly riotous, gathering held at the Dorchester for the benefit of the Press. But when that broke up about 12.30 am Philip moved on to a private room at The Belfry, a club off Belgrave Square, for another party to which the press was not invited. With a lot of young Navy and ex-Navy types present, including Mike Parker and David Milford Haven, best man as well as cousin for the occasion of the wedding, this was altogether a more hilarious affair, at least judging from a series of newspaper articles published over the name of Philip's cousin some years after. 'We celebrated the passing of one more good fellow into the state of matrimony with all the traditional rites and customs.'

The party went on into the early hours 'while the brandy circulated and the cigar smoke grew thicker than the speech of the raconteurs'. No wonder Philip overslept slightly on his wedding morn. Was there also the suggestion of a slight hangover and the need for a 'stabiliser'? It was hinted that there was. 'After careful consultation, we consumed only one glass of light sherry apiece after breakfast. We felt that by mid-morning the effects of this tonic would have dispersed the results of the night before.'

Despite this, Philip was ready on time, spruce in naval uniform, medals and Garter sash reinforced by the dress sword of his Battenberg grandfather which Uncle Dickie had loaned him. The best man was dying for a smoke, but was out of cigarettes. Philip had given up smoking and could not help out. So David concealed his best man's outfit under an old raincoat and cycled to Kensington High Street to replenish his own supply. Even after that, there was still time in hand. Bridegroom and best man strolled out once to the waiting car, but the duty policeman consulted his watch and shook his head. So they went back in again.

When they did finally get going they realised that they were both wearing identical naval caps. David's was bigger and, were there any confusion, Philip would be seen with a cap coming down over his ears. So they made an ink mark inside David's cap to enable them to tell one from the other.

'Thank goodness that's over,' Philip sighed to John Dean, the Mountbatten butler-turned-valet, after the wedding ceremony. There was a wedding 'breakfast' in the state supper room at the palace, then it was into one of the state landaus for the ceremonial drive to Waterloo station where the bridal train was waiting. Cheering crowds lined the route and Philip was happily waving back to them when there was a warning nudge from the bride. They were in Whitehall and she knew the royal ropes better than he did. The nudge came in the nick of time and he left off waving to bring his hand up in a crisp salute as the landau passed the Cenotaph.

They went off on honeymoon. Despite his new suits, shirts, shoes, Philip took along only two suitcases, one large, one small. Brides are different, of course, and it took fifteen cases to hold everything Elizabeth took on honeymoon with her. She also took along her pet corgi, Susan.

Married Life

Philip's Mountbatten relatives lent him Broadlands, their country mansion in Hampshire, for the first part of the honeymoon. To Philip's chagrin, sightseers flocked to the area by the bus-load and photographers lurked everywhere with their cameras. On Sunday morning, when he and Elizabeth went to Romsey Abbey, the service was frequently interrupted as more and more people pushed their way in. Outside in the churchyard, people pushed and jostled, and climbed on chairs and ladders to peer in at the windows. Even a sideboard was dragged into the churchyard to serve as a viewing platform. Philip was largely responsible for framing an ambiguous thank-you message in which reference was made to 'an unforgettable send-off' and to the loving interest of the public leaving 'an impression which will never grow faint'. The second part of the honeymoon, spent at Birkhall on the royal Balmoral estate, was less of a peep-show but hardly more romantic. Philip developed a head cold.

If the King had made Philip's secondary role abundantly clear in awarding him the Garter, Parliament did the same in the matter of state allowances. Elizabeth got £50,000 a year and Philip £10,000, which was only one-third as much as a Victorian Parliament had voted Albert (and an even smaller proportion in real terms). Still, it was a lot more than he was getting from the Navy.

For almost all of his twenty-six years Philip had been shuttled around between various boarding schools, relatives, ships. Ships' cabins and school dormitories had served as substitute homes. 'I've never really had a home,' he told a friend around the time of his marriage. 'Not since I was eight.' It was something he had long longed for. Even as a child, his cousin, Queen Alexandra, remembers, he had talked of the day when he would have a home of his own, using a stick to sketch a floor-plan of his dream-home, a country house, in the sand.

Sunninghill Park near Ascot, a royal grace-and-favour residence in which King George VI offered the newlyweds a wing, was a country house all right, but in need of extensive renovation. The work was put in hand, but the place was gutted by fire long before it could be completed.

As a stop-gap measure, lacking any other home, he and Elizabeth moved in next door to his grandmother and mother at Kensington Palace. The apartment, known as The Clock House, was loaned to them by the Earl and Countess of Athlone while they were away in South Africa. They had a staff of three, John Dean, a young footman named Cyril Dickman (still with them today as Palace Steward) and 'Bobo' MacDonald.

Margaret MacDonald – 'Only the Queen calls me Bobo,' she once reprimanded a royal aide – had already been with Elizabeth at that time for more than twenty of the girl's twenty-one years, serving her in turn as nurserymaid, nanny, personal maid. In childhood she had been almost like a second mother to her, bathing her, dressing her, playing with her, taking her for outings. Between the two of them, Princess and servant, there had developed a close and special relationship. It was to 'Bobo' that Elizabeth first confided her love for Philip. She had sympathised with her young charge throughout the long period of courtship, enjoying at second hand all the romantic joys of young love. But now that Lilibet, as she called the Princess, was actually married, it was as though she resented the fact that someone else had intervened in the intimate relationship she had so long shared with her. As far as Philip was concerned, the feeling was mutual. Elizabeth's mother may not have minded the cloyingly close relationship which had developed between Princess and servant; she may not even have noticed it. Philip did.

Nor was that the only problem which came his way during the early months of marriage. Elizabeth was soon pregnant and her father, when he was told, was eager that his first grandchild should be born at Buckingham Palace. So Philip found himself moving in with his in-laws, although Buckingham Palace was large enough for the newlyweds to have their own apartment. But they saw a lot of Elizabeth's parents and took quite a few of their meals with them.

Philip could consider himself fortunate in his in-laws. By and large, he got along extremely well with the King, though he was always a little in awe of him. He got along even better with his mother-in-law. He was at that time, and for some years to come, a breezy, immensely high-spirited young man, addicted to Navy-type skylarking and schoolboyish practical jokes. If the King, not always the most even-tempered of men, sometimes looked askance at his son-in-law's high jinks, the Queen (as the Queen Mother was then) enjoyed them immensely, even when she was on the receiving end. As when she left the room for a few minutes in the middle of a game of what some people call 'solitaire' and others 'patience.' When she returned and resumed the game, it seemed that nothing would go right. As she struggled to work out what had gone wrong she spotted Philip's grin. 'I know,' she said. 'You fixed the cards, Philip.'

Despite the fact that they did not yet have a home of their own, and other problems, the newlyweds were ecstatically happy. Philip, with his off-beat manner and boisterous ways, brought a new and totally different dimension into Elizabeth's hitherto cloistered and straitlaced life, and she responded to it. His practical joking delighted her even more than it did her mother. She was hardly the most physically active of young women – 'You have to run for the ball,' her tennis coach had once been obliged to point out – but Philip coerced her into two-handed games of cricket played with a soft ball in the palace gardens. If outings to nightclubs and theatres had to be cut because of the attention they attracted, there was the occasional private party to be enjoyed. Philip dressed up as a policeman, capering about with a pair of handcuffs (Elizabeth was the Spanish Infanta), for a fancy dress ball given by his cousin, Princess Marina. On another fancy dress occasion, with Parker completing the trio, they were decked out as the waiter, the porter and the upstairs maid.

As a weekend retreat they rented Windlesham Moor near Ascot. Philip, at this time, very much wanted to be the bread-winner and do the paying. So Ernest King, their butler at Windlesham Moor, found that he was expected to cope almost singlehanded with the house-warming party. 'What about the washing-up?' he wanted to know. 'Oh, Usher can help with that,' Philip replied, airily. Detective Inspector Usher was Elizabeth's security man. If Philip felt at the time that he wanted to be his own man and could not afford more staff out of his £10,000 a year, he had to give ground later. Two footmen were taken on at Windlesham Moor, with Elizabeth paying their wages.

Until now, Philip had been a big eater. But suddenly he decided it was necessary to start watching his weight. He took his early morning cup of tea, a habit he had developed in the Navy, without sugar; cut down to coffee and toast for breakfast. He exercised strenuously, swam in the palace pool, played squash with Mike Parker and jogged round the grounds at Windlesham Moor. He thought that golf might help him keep fit and tried it, but quickly gave it up again as being 'too tame'. Instead, he organised his own cricket team of gardeners, chauffeurs, detectives for games against visiting sides.

Having his own home for the first time also gave him a chance of making amends to his sisters for the way they had been slighted at the time of the wedding. He invited Sophie for a holiday at Windlesham Moor along with her two teenage daughters, his nieces, Christina and Dorothea. Another sister, Theodora – Philip called her 'Dolla' – also came to stay that summer with her daughter Margarita and son Max.

It was by no means all play and no work, of course. The Navy had fixed Philip up with a desk job in the Operations Division at the Admiralty to which he went back and forth like any other young husband. Well, perhaps not quite. There was time off for the growing number of royal chores he was required to undertake in his junior role as the King's son-in-law. He visited Broadcas*
ing House and presented the prizes at the London Boys' Cl·

Boxing Championships. He took his seat in the House of Lords; was installed as a Freeman of the City in both London and Edinburgh. Along with his bride, he found himself on public display in Cardiff, Coventry, Oxford and elsewhere.

Travelling together, attending the same functions, they were scarcely apart during that first year of marriage, though Philip, anxious that royal chores should not prevent him forging ahead with his naval career, did 'live in' briefly at the Royal Naval College, Greenwhich, while taking a staff course there. Others on the course were similarly living in and he had no desire either to enjoy special privilege or be the odd man out.

There was an official visit to Paris where Elizabeth, pregnant, swayed unsteadily while laying a wreath at the Arc de Triomphe. Frightened that she was going to faint, Philip moved in quickly to support and steady her. The stress of that visit at a time when Elizabeth was pregnant resulted in Philip having an attack of jaundice. It was not to be the only time he was to be similarly afflicted on stressful occasions. Nevertheless, he forced himself to carry on, though that was not the reason the French awarded him the Croix de Guerre with Palm during the course of the visit. It was during this visit that the British Embassy took over a nightclub for a private party, staging a floor show which was mild by Parisian standards. This did not prevent a parson back in Britain criticising the royal attendance at such a function as being 'a dark day in our history,' as though the pair had been indulging in a Roman orgy. It was the first time there had been any real criticism of the newlyweds and Philip was angry, though as much on his wife's account as on his own.

He was even angrier over an incident which occurred two nights before the baby was born. He and Elizabeth had been out to dinner with his cousin, Lady Brabourne, and her husband. Philip, as usual, took the wheel for the drive back to Buckingham Palace. Photographers' flashbulbs, exploding in the darkness as he headed between the palace gates, momentarily blinded him. He swerved and almost hit one of the pillars. He was livid as he climbed out of the car and stalked into the palace. 'Bloody fools might have caused an accident.' It was an incident which did nothing to alleviate his distrust and suspicion of photographers.

His dislike of photographers would seem to have grown with the years, though Philip himself does not see it in quite that way. He has always denied that he was responsible for pressing the button which resulted in two stalking photographers being sprayed with water at the Chelsea Flower Show. But so have the two men who were showing him round. 'I know I am accused of being nasty to photographers,' he once said. 'Actually, I am not. But if they poke a long lens into my private life, I am bloody nasty.' His track record does not entirely support his words. He has been 'bloody nasty' to photographers on occasions which were hardly part of his private life. 'Bloody lousy photographers', he called a group of them in Sweden. 'I hope he breaks his bloody neck,' he said when a Pakistani photographer, pole-climbing in the hope of a better picture, lost his grip and fell back into the crowd. 'Bad luck – I'm not dead,' he told converging photographers after gashing his chin on a bridle buckle during a polo game. In Brazil there was a hint that he had perhaps employed some rather strong language. One reporter, who had lip-read the remark, sought official confirmation of what the Consort had said. He was informed: 'Prince Philip was speaking French.' All of which was duly reported. 'I didn't know Prince Philip spoke French,' the Queen observed, slyly, when the report was brought to her attention.

For years, a freelance photographer named Ray Bellisario, specialising in candid camera shots of the Royals, was Philip's particular *bête noir*. Wherever Philip went at this time, Bellisario and his equipment were seldom far away. 'Get him and his bloody cameras out of here', Philip would order whenever the two of them ran into each other. One encounter between them, while Philip was sailing his ocean racer *Bloodhound* through the Scottish lochs, resulted in a series of quite heated exchanges between the Consort on deck and the photographer on shore.

Philip played squash with Michael Parker the night Prince Charles was born. Afterwards the pair of them had a dip in the palace pool and Philip was in the act of dressing when word reached him that he had a son. For a moment emotion robbed him of words. Then, shirt-sleeved, he dashed off in search of the flowers he had ordered earlier as a gift for his wife. He took them along to her and gazed in fascination at his son and her heir. His father-in-law shook hands and congratulated him; his mother-in-law embraced him warmly. 'Isn't it wonderful?' she said.

Philip, at that time, already knew something which had so far been kept hidden from Elizabeth. The King's health was beginning to fail. Cramp in the legs, experienced during the traditional summer stay at Balmoral, had been the first sign. Royal physicians had diagnosed arteriosclerosis, obstruction of the arteries. Sooner or later an operation would be necessary. Philip had been told, but cautioned not to mention the gravity of the King's condition to his wife. 'I don't want Lilibet worried before the baby is born,' said her father.

But this was a time for celebration, not sadness. Champagne corks popped. Michael Parker and Lieutenant General Sir Frederick Browning joined Philip in a toast to the baby. Philip was as excited as any of his aides have ever seen him. Spotting a couple of footmen passing the door, he sent Browning after them to call them into the room. He thrust champagne glasses into their hands. 'Drink up,' he said, excitedly. 'Wet the baby's head.'

Home – And Away

The birth of his son made Philip more eager than ever for a home of his own. A proper home, not a mere weekend place like Windlesham Moor. Work on renovating Clarence House, just along the road from Buckingham Palace, had already started and almost every day, and sometimes twice a day, he went along there to check on progress. Despite his urgings, it was the following summer before the place was ready. He and Elizabeth moved in finally on 4 July and Philip could not resist a wisecrack about it being 'Independence Day'.

They furnished the house mainly with wedding gifts. If the decor largely reflected Elizabeth's taste, Philip's influence was also apparent. He was responsible for the Norman Wilkinson seascapes which hung in the entrance hall and for the cartoons by Giles, Bateman and Osbert Lancaster which adorned one of the corridors. 'My art collection,' he said of the cartoons and has gone on to collect many more since, including some of which he is the butt. If he did not have a dressing room like a ship's cabin, as Uncle Dickie did, he did have a study which reflected something of his personality, maple panelled walls (the panelling was a wedding gift from Canada) which hid store cupboards, with a let-down section adjoining his desk to provide an extra working surface, and a bookcase which opened to reveal a concealed filing cabinet.

He was very much the family man, even helping to bath baby Charles, though bath-time when Philip lent a hand tended to become very much a splashing playtime dominated by toy boats – what else? – and even a toy diver who could be made to descend into the bath-water by squeezing a rubber bulb. A friend asked what the baby was like. 'A plum pudding,' Philip replied, laughing.

There were more visits to various parts of Britain, more public appearances in Lancashire, Wales, Northern Ireland, Yorkshire, Derbyshire, Nottinghamshire. There was a visit to the Channel Isles with the weather turning really rough as they headed for Sark in HMS *Anson*. Elizabeth was seasick and Philip wondered if she was fit enough to go ashore. She insisted that she was and climbed down into the waiting boat. But at the quayside, with the boat heaving and sinking with the waves, she could not quite make it onto dry land. Twice she tried and twice she failed. Behind her back, Philip signalled to 'Boy' Browning, who was on the quayside and, as the boat lifted yet again, gave his wife a push which sent her staggering into Browning's waiting arms.

What was really needed, it was felt in the family circle, was something which would enable Philip to make a real impact on public consciousness. So Uncle Dickie obligingly stepped down from his post as president of the National Playing Fields Association to enable Philip to take over. By arrangement with the Navy, he went on half-pay so that he could put in a more or less regular 9–5 working day at the Association's head office. 'I have no intention of being a sitting tenant,' he said when he took over the presidency, and proved it by addressing envelopes and sticking on stamps. More importantly, he launched the Association's silver jubilee fund with a target of half-a-million pounds. He announced that he would 'go anywhere, do anything' if it resulted in a new playing field. And he did. He went to boxing matches and holiday camps, entertained publicans at the palace and attended the Butlin's reunion at the Albert Hall. He coaxed such a varied assortment as Bob Hope, Frank Sinatra, boxing promoter Jack Solomons and the US 32nd Infantry Band into doing their bit for the cause. He himself played in cricket matches. He was both a keen player and fan at the time, driving with his car radio tuned in to the England–Australia games. At the crucial stage of one game he even had a portable radio in his carriage to keep him in touch with events as he participated in the traditional state drive at Royal Ascot. And hardly had he reached the royal box than he vanished into the privacy of the rear room to watch the game on television. His participation in matches to raise funds for the Association resulted in crowds of near-Test match proportions. There were, for instance, 25,000 spectators for a match at Arundel Castle in 1953, when he was still working for the Association.

It was not simply a young man's enthusiasm for something new, though it was that, too, of course. He has been the same with every cause with which he has been associated. The end, he believes, justifies the means. So when, on one occasion in America, there was an offer of $100,000 if he would change into swimming trunks and take a dip in a private pool, he did just that. Undignified for a royal prince? Philip wouldn't agree.

His early work for the Association was a foretaste of what was to come. His later use of television for various causes and to enhance the royal image was foreshadowed by his appearance in an NPFA appeal film. He was so tense he could not control the jittering of one leg and the cameraman had to work from an angle which would not betray him. Visiting Edinburgh to link up with the Scottish Playing Fields Association, he walked in procession to church, inspected three guards of honour, took the salute at an army parade, lunched with the Lord Provost, watched a fly-past and visited a local seamen's club – a packed programme which was to be echoed many times in his role of Consort.

When he took over the Association presidency, an average of thirty new playing fields a year was being created. Within three years the average annual number was 300. Within ten years an additional million pounds had been raised and spent, a staggering total of 2,500 new playing fields had been opened and Philip was having to use closed circuit television to open yet more, five at a time.

Philip, who had always longed for a home of his own, now had one. Having accomplished this, he felt a sudden urge to return to his old love – the sea. So he resumed his naval career and was posted to Malta as first lieutenant aboard *Chequers*, leader of the First Mediterranean Destroyer Flotilla. His pay of £1. 6s. (£1.30)

6

a day was augmented by 18/6d (93p) marriage allowance, which worked out at slightly over £15 a week. Early on, there was some slight problem between Philip and his commanding officer as to which of them should call the other 'Sir!' Both thought it a title due to the other and in the end Philip got his way. A somewhat similar problem cropped up when he took his Command Examinations a little later. To his own surprise – and everyone else's – he failed in Torpedo & ASDIC, which he thought of as perhaps his best subject. Admiral Sir Arthur Power, the Mediterranean Commander in Chief, was not only surprised, but perturbed. 'If they try to fix it, I'll quit the Navy,' Philip threatened. But they – whoever *they* were – did not. He sat the examination a second time and this time he passed.

Elizabeth flew out to join him for their second wedding anniversary and stayed on over Christmas. It was like a second honeymoon. Better. The weather in Malta was certainly a distinct improvement. They stayed with Philip's Mountbatten uncle and aunt – Earl Mountbatten was vice admiral commanding the First Cruiser Squadron at the time – at the Villa Guardamangia, later renting it for themselves. In Philip's spells off-duty they went sailing and fishing together. Philip also enjoyed himself swimming, water-skiing and sub-aqua diving. There were picnics in deserted coves and dancing at a local hotel. It was all very romantic and it is perhaps not to be wondered at that Elizabeth became pregnant again.

Uncle Dickie was a keen polo player and Philip caught his enthusiasm. Elizabeth bought him his first polo pony as a Christmas gift, and sometimes wished that she hadn't. Philip always played a very aggressive game, as much dash as skill, and in those days he was also a beginner. Inevitably there were times when he was unseated and hit the ground pretty heavily, causing the watching Elizabeth to spring anxiously to her feet, her face pale with alarm. As addicted as ever to skylarking, he was with other polo players exercising their ponies the day Royal Marines staged a landing exercise on the island. Pointing their polo sticks like lances, the polo players promptly charged the landing Marines with wild cries of 'We are the Knights of Malta'. Philip found himself on the carpet for that particular escapade.

Elizabeth flew out to join him again for her birthday in April and he returned to London later to be with her for Anne's birth. He invited his eldest sister, Margarita, to be Anne's godmother (Uncle Dickie was another of the godparents), but she could not afford the air fare to London. She and her husband were having a hard time of it in postwar Germany. To make ends meet, they opened their castle at Langenburg to the public, served strawberry teas in the rose garden and took in paying guests. So Philip paid her fare for her.

He was posing for a miniature by Australian-born Stella Marks, to be added to Elizabeth's collection of family miniatures, when news of Anne's birth brought the sitting to an abrupt end. Philip personally registered the baby's birth and was solemnly handed the identity card and ration book, orange juice and cod liver oil which were the birthright of every baby at the time.

He was promoted to lieutenant commander and given command of the frigate *Magpie*. Being who he was, *Magpie* immediately became as much a floating embassy as a naval frigate. Some people referred to it, cuttingly, as 'Edinburgh's private yacht', but Philip did only what was asked of him. With the King's health failing rapidly, he helped out in the Mediterranean and the Middle East just as Elizabeth was doing back home. He opened the Gibraltar Legislative Council, made formal calls on King Ibn Saud of Saudi Arabia, King Abdullah of Jordan and President Jehal Bayar of Turkey, who gave him three more polo ponies. Other gifts and acquisitions over the next few years were to see him with a string of over a dozen ponies at one time. Uncle Dickie slotted him into his Shrimps team for a cup match against the Optimists, with uncle and nephew contributing two goals apiece to their team's 8–0 victory. He played for the Navy against Rome and against the Middle East Land Forces. Playing for Destroyer Command against the Royal Artillery he was again thrown. As Elizabeth came to her feet in alarm, he cantered over to her, shirt torn, elbow bleeding. 'Nothing to worry about. Just a scratch.'

She had again flown out to be with him. Together, they paid a call on the Italian president and also saw the Pope, something which did not go down too well in all quarters back home. Goodness only knows what would have been said if they had accepted an invitation received around around this time to visit Philip's sisters in Germany. Sensibly, Philip realised that that would not be possible so soon after the war.

There was a cruise to Greece with Philip in *Magpie* and Elizabeth, because the frigate did not have adequate accommodation for her, in HMS *Surprise*. Michael Parker was aboard *Surprise* with her in his role of equerry and he and Philip indulged in the old naval signalling game: –

Surprise to *Magpie*: Princess full of beans.

Magpie to *Surprise*: Is that the best you can give her?

It gave Philip a considerable degree of satisfaction that Greece, which had hounded his father into exile, should now welcome the son back with booming guns and cheering crowds. They stayed at the royal palace in Athens with Philip's cousin Paul, now King Paul, and his wife Frederika.

As always, during that tour of duty, Philip was concerned that any ship he was aboard should be the best there was. 'He worked us like dogs and treated us like gentlemen,' one of *Magpie*'s ratings remembers. And if he drove his men hard, he drove himself every bit as hard. He had earlier played for *Chequers* against *Forth* at hockey and won the javelin event with a throw of 115 feet in an athletics contest against the Malta Pegasus Club. Now, as skipper of *Magpie*, he stripped to the waist to row stroke in the annual naval regatta and had the satisfaction of seeing the frigate's crew win six out of ten events. At the end of the day he hoisted a red plywood cock as symbol that *Magpie* was the cock ship of the 2nd Frigate Flotilla.

His pint-sized cabin aboard *Magpie* also did duty as an office from which, between naval duties, he continued his efforts on behalf of the National Playing Fields Association as well as plugging away at the speech he was to make shortly as the new president of the British Association for the Advancement of Science. He drafted the speech on naval signal pads and spent seven months researching and perfecting it. He dragged in everything from reaping machines to synthetic fibres and aniline dyes, so that the finished speech became a sort of forerunner of James Burke's *Connections* – except that Philip was speaking not for popular consumption but to trained scientific minds. 'A most discerning survey', Sir Harold Hartley was to call it. It would have been even more discerning – and certainly more controversial – had Philip not shown the speech to his father-in-law in advance. The King thought he should cut out a reference to the suppression of inventions in order to maintain obsolete equipment. He did as the King suggested.

With the King's health failing further, Philip's time in the Navy was fast running out. It became necessary for Elizabeth to deputise for her father on many occasions and she felt she needed Philip's help and support more and more. There was a royal tour of Canada in the planning stage, too, but the King was now too ill to undertake it. He wanted Elizabeth and Philip to go instead.

The call to take over had come sooner than Philip had anticipated and earlier than he would have wished. But he was the husband of the future Queen and so there was no choice. Reluctantly he said goodbye to the crew of *Magpie*. 'It will be a long time before I want those again,' he said as his valet stowed away his uniforms. But if he had any lingering hope that circumstances might one day permit him to resume his naval career, he was to be disappointed. He would go to sea again, but not as a serving officer – and only a model of his old command, in a showcase aboard the royal yacht, would serve to remind him of his Navy life.

'Awful News'

It was originally planned that Elizabeth and Philip should go to Canada by sea, but those plans had to be abandoned as the King's health deteriorated further and cancer was diagnosed. Further surgery, in the form of a lung resection, was necessary. As heir to the throne, Elizabeth could not leave the country until it was known that the operation had been successful. As a daughter, she had no wish to leave until she knew her father was all right By the time it was known that the King was safely through the operation it was too late to get to Canada on time. The tour could still go ahead, but the schedule and timing would have to be completely changed.

'If we fly there would be no need to change anything,' Philip suggested.

For the heir to the throne to fly the Atlantic was a novel idea in 1951, however commonplace similar flights have become since. And risky, the Cabinet thought. The King's operation had gone well, but he was still seriously ill. What if his successor should meet with an accident? But Philip urged his point and finally prime minister Clement Attlee gave them the go-ahead. They flew from London to Montreal in a BOAC Stratocruiser.

It was Philip's first major royal tour; a total of over 16,000 miles with seventy stops embracing every Canadian province in addition in two days spent visiting President Truman in Washington. He found himself shaking hands at the rate of 2,000 a week (1,800 on a single day in Washington). Even without complications, he would probably have found it something of a strain. And there were plenty of complications. The King was still gravely ill – so ill that Elizabeth took with her to Canada a large sealed envelope containing the accession declaration she would have to make and instructions as to all else she must do if her father died in her absence. Naturally, she was worried about him, and Philip was worried about her. In every possible way he tried to lessen the strain on her. He tried to ensure that she got enough rest. If her spirits seemed to flag, he buoyed them with a joke and was quick to step in with a witticism if she dried up in conversation. Every day she telephoned London to find out how her father was. The news was mainly cheering, but she may have felt that she was not being told the whole truth. Philip's love of practical joking sometimes helped to relieve the tension. For breakfast one morning he fed her imitation bread rolls which squeaked when bitten. He gave her a can labelled 'Mixed Nuts' from which an imitation snake popped out when she opened it and, on another occasion, chased her through the royal train wearing a set of horrendous false teeth.

But the double strain of the tour itself and of constantly having to bolster his wife's spirits told on him. Occasionally his temper snapped. Photographers got some of the backwash. 'What are they belly-aching about now?' he demanded, when photographers at Niagara who had missed the picture of him in waterproof gear wanted him to climb into it all over again. And at Ottawa, when a flashbulb exploded close to Elizabeth, Philip glared at the photographer so ferociously that the wretched man backed off in alarm. When things went wrong it was not always Philip's fault, of course. His refusal, in Montreal, to eat lunch while a thousand spectators looked on was perhaps not unreasonable. Charles II may have enjoyed having people watch him eat; Philip doesn't and he insisted on a private room. And it was surely understandable that he should grumble 'This is a waste of time' when he found himself shaking hands with the same people twice over at a press reception. In Vancouver, the inevitable Indian princess popped up unexpectedly from somewhere seeking to be presented to the Queen. No such presentation was listed in their itinerary and Philip was not happy

[87]

at adding to Elizabeth's already full schedule. Nevertheless the presentation took place.

But such small upsets were more than offset by other occasions, for example when Philip waved dignitaries and entourage to one side so that a small boy could get a good snapshot of Elizabeth. By fun events like the square dance which also cropped up unexpectedly in their schedule. Philip sent his valet out to buy a check shirt and a pair of jeans and danced still sporting the price tag. More important things like the plastic bubble which was fitted to their car so that the crowds could see them clearly even in bad weather. It was Philip's inventive brain which came up with that idea. All in all, Philip's first major tour – Elizabeth had already toured South Africa with her parents – was a major success. His father-in-law was delighted. So delighted – he was especially pleased to receive a letter from President Truman praising his daughter and son-in-law as 'a lovely young lady and her personable husband' – that on their return he made both of them members of the Privy Council.

But hardly were they back home, it seemed, than they were packing to leave again. This time, again deputising for the sick King, on a planned tour of Australia and New Zealand. It is history that they never got there.

With the rest of the Royals, Philip went to Sandringham for Christmas. It was not the happiest of occasions. Illness and operation had left the King so weak that he had to hand out his Christmas gifts while seated in an armchair. He could not climb the stairs and a bedroom was made up for him on the ground floor. He did not even have the strength to join in when the rest of the family sang carols around the grand piano. After Christmas, however, he seemed to take a turn for the better. 'I'll soon be able to shoot again, I think,' he said to Philip one day, lifting his walking stick to his shoulder and pointing it like a gun. In fact, he and Philip did go shooting together on 24 January, through the coverts of Church Farm and the fields known as Eleven Acres. And ill though he undoubtedly still was, the King insisted on travelling back to London with Elizabeth and Philip to see them off. As a farewell treat he took them to see the American musical

South Pacific. Philip's last glimpse of him was on the tarmac at London airport, looking haggard and drawn as he waved good-bye.

They flew first to Nairobi where they carried out a few official engagements before going to the Sagana Royal Lodge, another of their many wedding gifts, where they planned to relax for a few days before boarding the liner *Gothic* at Mombasa. During the brief time they were there they went riding together and Philip did some fishing along the Sagana river. They spent a night together at Treetops, in those days no more than a small hunting lodge built into the giant branches of a fig tree, watching and photographing the game which came to drink at the water-hole below.

Back at the lodge the following morning, Philip was indulging in a brief cat-nap when there was a tap on the door. It was Michael Parker. That he was the bearer of grave news was written on his face.

'I'm afraid there's some awful news,' he said. 'The King is dead.'

Word of the King's death had reached the lodge in curiously roundabout fashion. The *East African Standard* received it first in the form of a Reuter newsflash. Even as the newsflash was being received the paper had put in a call to its man covering the royal visit, Granville Roberts. Roberts had taken the call in a telephone box at the Outspan Hotel in Nyeri where, by chance, Martin Charteris, Private Secretary to the Princess, also happened to be lunching that day. Together, the two of them had telephoned the lodge, where Parker took the call. That was perhaps half an hour earlier. Parker had been trying ever since to obtain official confirmation of the King's death, but had been unable to get through to Government House in Nairobi. However, he had also had the forethought to switch on a radio and confirmation had eventually come in the form of a brief newscast interrupting the scheduled programme.

Philip was deeply affected by the news of the King's death. Slightly in awe though he had always been of his father-in-law, he had been fond of him, too. More now than ever he knew that

Elizabeth, always so close to her father, would need a husband's support and sympathy. Ashen-faced, he went in search of her to break the news of her father's death.

Husband Of The Queen

With three such efficient organisers as Philip, Charteris and Parker in the party, it was no more than a matter of hours before the new royal show was on the road. Handicapped though they were in making arrangements by the fact that only a single telephone line linked the Sagana Royal Lodge with the outside world, by six o'clock that evening they were driving along the rust-red road which led to Nanyuki on the first stage of the journey home. In the rush of departure, inevitably a few things were overlooked; Philip left his field-glasses behind at the lodge.

At Nanyuki they squeezed into an unpressurised Dakota hastily laid on by East African Airlines for the flight to Entebbe where they re-boarded the Argonaut which had flown them out and which, as chance had it, was still standing by to take any surplus baggage back to Britan. They arrived back at their Clarence House home to find one of the famous royal Boxes already awaiting Elizabeth's attention. Leather-covered, locked, still labelled 'The King' in gold letters (there had not yet been time to substitute 'The Queen'), it was the first of an endless succession which have pursued her throughout her years of monarchy. More than anything else, that Box forced home upon Philip the dramatic change which had taken place in Elizabeth's status . . . and his own very secondary role. Griefstricken though she was over her father's death, she had to cope with the contents of the Box alone. Philip would willingly have spared her the burden, but was not permitted to see the state papers, Foreign Office telegrams, Commonwealth communications and suchlike, that it held. And he is still not today. Victoria's Consort, Albert, may have dealt with the contents of the Boxes, drafting replies, comments and criticisms which his royal wife fair-copied in her own hand, but times have changed since Victoria's day. Victoria, at the outset of her reign, had no Private Secretary to advise her – that office became the influential one it is today only after Albert's death – and it was Albert who came to act as her Private Secretary and much else. Indeed, in some respects he acted almost as King. Philip's role, as he quickly discovered, was to be very different, more delicate and more difficult for a man of his nature.

His new nebulous role of Consort was underlined by what happened the morning following their return. They were together, as they had so often been on public occasions, as they walked through from Clarence House to St James's Palace where Elizabeth was to make her Declaration of Accession. But once there, tradition required that he leave her to stand alone while he, as a Privy Councillor, took his place among all the other members of the Accession Council. It was further emphasised by what happened at the state opening of Parliament later that year. The Queen's parents had always sat side by side on two thrones for this top ceremonial occasion. But following the death of the King, one of those thrones was whipped speedily away and Philip, that first year, found himself relegated to a chair of state one step down from the throne occupied by his wife. 'The part the Duke of Edinburgh will play will be that of a husband supporting his wife,' explained the Lord Chancellor's office. Later, the second throne was to be restored. So perhaps the new Queen had echoed her great-great-grandmother's words: 'It is a strange omission in the Constitution that while the wife of a King has the highest rank and dignity in the Realm assigned to her by law, the husband of a Queen regnant is entirely ignored.'

Philip must have been horrified to learn that not only was he classed as holding an 'office of profit under the Crown' but what that office of profit was – 'husband of the Queen.' The wonder is that he was not listed merely as 'father of the Queen's children.'

Despite some arguments to the contrary based on some parts

of constitutional law, Philip himself thinks that Elizabeth, by marrying him, took his name of Mountbatten. If so, then she was a Mountbatten when she ascended the throne. His Uncle Dickie, arrogantly proud of the long Mountbatten-Battenberg lineage, took the same viewpoint. So, it would seem, did Winston Churchill, prime minister at the time of the Queen's accession, and Sir Alan Lascelles, the Private Secretary she inherited from her father. And between Churchill and Mountbatten there was little love lost.

It was at Churchill's insistence and on the advice of Lascelles that, two months after her accession, the new Queen issued an Order in Council declaring it to be her 'Will and Pleasure that I and my children shall be styled and known as the House and Family of Windsor and that my descendants, other than female descendants who marry and their descendants, shall bear the name of Windsor.'.

Philip was not exactly enthused at the thought that his children would no longer bear their father's name of Mountbatten – an adopted name, true, but then so was the royal name of Windsor – but he made no great song and dance about it. He was hardly in a position to do so, though he did suggest a compromise formula: The Family of Windsor of the House of Edinburgh. That got rid of the Mountbatten name which seemed to be the main issue. However, even that was not acceptable to those who advised the new, young Queen.

Few things, in fact, went Philip's way during that early phase of his wife's Monarchy. Clarence House had been his first real home, a happy home, and he would have preferred to have gone on living there, leaving Buckingham Palace to be used as the office building of Monarchy. He had had one brief experience of living at the palace and was inclined to share the views of previous royal occupants that it was a cross between a sepulchre and an icebox. Elizabeth, too, would have been happy to stay on at Clarence House, but Churchill would not have it. It was unthinkable for the Monarch not to live at Buckingham Palace, he insisted. So, the Easter following the Queen's accession they moved over and the palace promptly took them over.

Philip found that it was not only in size that Buckingham Palace differed from Clarence House, but in atmosphere. At Clarence House things had been relatively informal, with members of their small staff free to simply tap on a door and walk in if there was anything they wanted. At Buckingham Palace, as was quickly made clear, that would no longer be tolerated. It may seem odd that a royal page, inherited, like the Queen's Private Secretary, from her father, should set the standard, but that is what happened. Clarence House aides who moved over with them found that they had to contact the page first – 'You must be properly announced' – if they wanted to see the Queen.

'Anyone can still walk in and see me,' Philip said when he heard about this. But it was one thing for him to say it and quite another for others to buck the system. Most of those who had moved over with them from Clarence House quickly conformed with the new, more starchy protocol imposed by life at Buckingham Palace. Michael Parker was perhaps a rare exception. He would still stroll casually into Philip's study after simply tapping on the door and, in private at least, continue to address him informally by his first name (though careful to call him 'Sir' in the presence of others). But then Parker was an old and trusted friend, sharing a relationship which went back nearly a decade to their war-time naval days together, as privileged where Philip was concerned as Bobo MacDonald was with Elizabeth.

Elizabeth too had come to know and like Parker during his six years as equerry. She particularly enjoyed his refreshingly breezy outlook and lively sense of fun. He made her laugh, she said once.

But even Parker's breezy outlook and sense of fun could not always dispel the sense of gloom which descended upon Philip during that early phase of his wife's monarchy. There were too many other things which upset and frustrated him. He was irritated by the continuation of a tradition dating from the days of Queen Victoria which saw the Queen's Piper scrunching up and down beneath the dining room window at breakfast time, skirling Scottish airs on his bagpipes. He thought it ridiculous that footmen should rush around opening doors for him. 'I can do it. I've got hands, haven't I?' And he positively refused to go along with the longwinded chain of command which was involved merely to perform such a simple task as ordering a couple of late-night sandwiches. The system, he was told, was that he should inform his page who would pass on the information to the Comptroller of Supplies department which would then instruct a chef to prepare the sandwiches. The chef would contact a footman etc. This was all nonsense, Philip thought, and simply telephoned through direct to the kitchen.

A convenient weekend retreat, similar to that provided by Windlesham Moor when he and Elizabeth had previously lived at the palace, might have helped to ease his irritation. But there wasn't one. Royal Lodge might have served the purpose, but the Queen Mother, as she now was, was still using that. There was Windsor Castle, of course, but that was hardly a weekend cottage even by royal standards. Philip did try turning it into one, but the idea never quite worked out. He felt that four servants – a chef, a footman, Bobo MacDonald to look after Elizabeth and his own valet – were more than sufficient when they went there for the weekend. Buckingham Palace thought otherwise. Chefs did not prepare vegetables. Or make the coffee. Footmen did not clean the silver. Only a page could lay the royal table. And so it went on. In no time at all, Philip's four servants had grown to a retinue of fourteen and weekends at Windsor were simply like being at Buckingham Palace all over again.

The most frustrating part of it of all was the nebulous quality of his new role as Consort. No one seemed to know what he was supposed to do, only what he was *not* to do, and hardly anyone seemed to care. The lives of previous Consorts – there had been only four in history – offered little guidance and even less encouragement. Mary Tudor's Consort, Philip of Spain, was hardly in the country at all. William of Orange had made himself King to Mary's Queen which Philip had no desire to do and could not have done even if he had so wished. Queen Anne's Consort, Prince George of Denmark, seemed to have done very little more than sire a succession of seventeen children, none of whom survived into their teens.

Victoria's Consort, Albert, was a more recent example, but hardly more encouraging. 'The position of a Prince Consort requires that a husband should entirely sink his own individual existence in that of his wife,' wrote Albert. It was, of course, a dictum he had not scrupulously observed. Nor was it one a man of Philip's independent nature would find it at all easy to follow. But what was the answer? Unable to find one at first, frustrated, it seemed, at every turn, it was no wonder that Philip, shortly after the return to Buckingham Palace, developed another attack of jaundice which kept him in bed for three weeks. No wonder, too, that his sisters, on visits to Britain, found him depressed.

There were compensations, of course. Parliament increased his state allowance to £40,000 a year. A royal warrant issued by the Queen decreed that he should 'henceforth upon all occasions and in all meetings except where otherwise provided by Act of Parliament, have, hold and enjoy Place, Pre-eminence and Precedence next to Her Majesty.' First Gentleman of the Realm. Well, it was something. He was named as Regent (in place of Princess Margaret) with responsibility for overseeing the son who no longer bore his name in the event that Charles should succeed to the throne while still a minor. He was made one of the six Counsellors of State to act for the Queen if she was ill or out of the country.* As she has seldom been ill and Philip invariably accompanies her on overseas trips it is a role he has rarely, if ever, fulfilled. He was appointed an Admiral of the Fleet, a Field Marshal and a Marshal of the Royal Air Force.† Ordinary promotion in the course of a normal naval career would perhaps have meant more to him.

Some people did want him for himself, as he realised when Sir Leslie Hollis, Commandant General of the Royal Marines, called at the palace. The Marines, he told Philip, needed a new

* At present the other five are the Queen Mother, Prince Charles, Princess Anne, Princess Margaret and the Duke of Gloucester. Prince Andrew will take over from Gloucester at the age of twenty-one.
† See appendix IV.

Left: The one-year-old Prince Philip photographed in England in 1922.
(CAMERA PRESS, LONDON)

Above: Prince Philip the actor—seen here in the Gordonstoun school production of 'Macbeth'.
(FOX PHOTOS)

Left: The bearded Duke of Edinburgh during the Second World War.
(CAMERA PRESS, LONDON)

20th November 1947: The wedding of HRH Princess Elizabeth and HRH The Duke of Edinburgh. The marriage took place five years before the Princess succeeded to the throne on the death of her father, King George VI. (Baron/CAMERA PRESS, LONDON)

Left: During a Royal Tour of Nigeria, the Queen and Prince Philip enjoy a display of traditional dancing. Accompanying them are: (l. to r.) Dr Aziwike, Premier of Eastern Nigeria; Lady Euston, lady-in-waiting to the Queen; and Lieutenant-Commander Michael Parker, private secretary to the Prince. (David Moore/CAMERA PRESS, LONDON)

Below: Among the royal enthusiasts for the thrills of waterskiing, the Duke of Edinburgh was undoubtedly one of the first. (CAMERA PRESS, LONDON)

Right: Lieutenant-Commander the Duke of Edinburgh on board HMS Magpie during the Mediterranean Fleet's summer cruise in August 1951.
(CAMERA PRESS, LONDON)

Below: The polo-playing prince gallops his pony down the field, his polo stick raised high.
(Jack Esten/CAMERA PRESS, LONDON)

Above: A family get-together at Balmoral on the occasion of the Royal Silver Wedding. (l. to r.) The Duke of Edinburgh; the Queen; Prince Andrew (rear); Prince Edward; Princess Anne; Prince Charles. (Patrick Lichfield/CAMERA PRESS, LONDON)

Left: Royal Threesome: Prince Philip looks on, an amused bystander, whilst Prince Charles and the late Lord Mountbatten converse. (Arthur Edwards/ CAMERA PRESS, LONDON)

Right: In full protective headgear the Duke of Edinburgh inspects the construction of the Munich stadium for the 1972 Olympics.
(CAMERA PRESS, LONDON)

Below: A Man For All Seasons: Sheltered from the rain by a large umbrella, Prince Philip greets his guests at a Government House garden party in Sydney.
(Mitchell/Davey/ CAMERA PRESS, LONDON)

Above: Prince Philip inspects the pick of the thoroughbred Arab horses from King Feisal's stables in Riyadh.
(T. D. Marshall/CAMERA PRESS, LONDON)

Left: On tour in India, the Duke takes an interest in the work of village tailors.
(T. S. Satyan/CAMERA PRESS, LONDON)

Below: Making friends with some of the younger citizens of Montserrat—they have brought the Prince a basket of fruit.
(John Reader/CAMERA PRESS, LONDON)

Left: Behind the scenes:
Prince Philip, in prepar-
ation for his role as TV
personality, arranges props
and liaises closely with
cameramen.
(CAMERA PRESS, LONDON)

Left: As Patron of the
London Federation of Boys
Clubs, the Duke of Edin-
burgh meets some of the
boys at Hindleap Warren,
the Federation's per-
manent camp in Ashdown
Forest, Sussex.
(LONDON FEDERATION
OF BOYS' CLUBS)

Captain General to replace the late King. Philip assumed it was the Queen they wanted and was prepared to put it to her. Diplomatically, his visitor corrected the impression. 'We would like you, Sir.'

'This may be a little difficult', said Philip. But the following week, when the two men met again, he was able to tell Hollis, 'General, you've got me.'

With Elizabeth's accession to the throne, the relationship between her and Philip, as wife and husband, underwent a slight and subtle change. Previously Philip saw to the running of things in their married life, and Elizabeth had been content that he should do so. At Clarence House, things had been referred to him – not her – for decision. But now, even on things Philip could easily have dealt with, people preferred the decisions to come from the Queen. And Elizabeth, in her new role as Monarch, seemed to prefer it that way. New to the manifold duties of monarchy despite her apprenticeship as princess, she devoted the major part of her time and energy towards mastering the job. If she needed advice and guidance, she turned not to Philip, but to the top-level royal aides who had served her father before her, as, indeed, she was almost bound to do. If and when personal life clashed with the requirements of monarchy, then monarchy, she felt, came first. Philip could not be expected to see it altogether the same way. If his wife suddenly had too much to do, then he had too little that was important and meaningful to a man of his temperament.

Not that he was by any means without public work during this early phase of his wife's monarchy. He was already the active head of six organisations and honorary president of some thirty more when the Queen ascended the throne. Invitations were received to attend functions, make speeches etc, but they were nothing compared with the torrent which was to come later. He visited, among other places, the atomic research centre at Harwell, the Royal Aeronautical Establishment and the Chemical Research Laboratory at Teddington. He wrote his own speeches, enlivening them, as he had enlivened his lectures at Corsham, with a touch of wit. He told the Military College of

Science that the basic requirements for a good officer were the ability to handle men, the ability to handle machines and, these days, the ability to handle paper. He invited the Chartered Insurance Institute to let him have a policy providing coverage against 'excessive hospitality'. He was blunt as well as witty, calling road construction in Britain 'an absolute paradise for buck-passers' and telling the Society of Motor Manufacturers that it would not be long 'before it will be quicker to go on foot.'

He soon found out that it was not possible to please all the people all the time. He was labelled 'a royal meddler' by some for pointing out that national service helped to build character in the young and 'ignorant' when he tried to urge the military advantages of a new four-wheel drive vehicle.

In the reorganisation of rooms in the royal apartment which followed their return to Buckingham Palace, the Queen preferred to take over her mother's sitting room for use as a combination sitting room and study. This left the King's old room, high ceilinged, tall windowed, solidly furnished, free for Philip. He promptly set about making it more modern and businesslike with a press-button system which enabled him to operate tape recorder, television, even draw the curtains, without leaving his desk. Some palace officials viewed this sudden advent of twentieth century technology with considerable alarm. What in the world would the man do next? Better caution him, discreetly of course, not to muck about with the ornately carved plaster ceiling. Philip had no intention of mucking about with the ceiling. He simply had another ceiling installed lower down to give the room a more modern aspect. He hung a portrait of his mother over the fireplace flanked by portraits of his dead father and his Battenberg grandfather. A move to brighten the corridor outside with other paintings came to grief, however. The paintings were already hanging in place when the Queen first saw them. They were part of the Crown collection and had been transferred from one of the state rooms. 'You'll get us all shot,' Elizabeth chided her husband. Jokingly, of course. But back the paintings had to go.

In June, 1953, Philip had a dictagraph communications system installed in his study. A similar system was later to be

[98]

installed in the Queen's room and gradually, as Philip's ideas took root, amplifying and recording machines, photo-copiers, electric typewriters and revolving card-index systems were to pop up all over the palace. Philip's own index system, with its back-up micro-filming, today contains over 70,000 references, constantly updated, so that he knows who people are when he meets them and runs no risk of making the same sort of speech in the same place twice.

Like a good sailor, almost the first thing he did on moving into the palace was take his bearings, no easy task in a building containing hundreds of rooms (though perhaps not the 600 of legend, depending upon what you class as a room) and miles of red-carpeted corridor. He explored the whole place from basements to attics, losing his way several times in the process. In search of the Ministry of Works office on one occasion, he ended up in the basement coal cellars. Another time he accidentally butted in on a couple of housemaids enjoying tea and buns in one of the servants' sittings rooms which are scattered about the palace. 'Don't get up,' he grinned. 'I'm looking for the post office.'

Everywhere he went he asked probing questions. 'Some of his questions were the sort lots of us had wanted to ask for years,' recalls the then Deputy Comptroller of Supply. The answers he received to his questions sparked off a number of ideas for making the palace more efficient, more economic or both. But each idea, in turn, was to meet with stiff resistance from entrenched attitudes, and Philip in those days was not in a position to push things through. So his proposals that Buckingham Palace should have its own bakery and its own laundry, though both would probably have paid off in the long run, never got off the ground. They were vetoed on the grounds of capital outlay.

He had more, though by no means complete, success with his idea for a new kitchen. The existing kitchen, he felt, was too large, too old-fashioned and certainly too far from where the actual eating was done. As a result, food for the royal dining table had to be manhandled along corridors and up stairways on heated trolleys. Philip's idea, for family meals, was that there should be a small modern kitchen on the same floor as the royal apartment. This time he got approval and a convenient room was converted and fitted out with all the latest labour-saving culinary devices. But royal chefs, for reasons best known to themselves, seemed to prefer their old haunt and eventually drifted back there.

Defeated for the time being in his efforts to update Buckingham Palace, except where his own study was concerned, Philip turned his attention to Sandringham. This was his wife's private property, bought by George VI from his brother, the Duke of Windsor, following the Abdication, and left to her by her father. So there were no Government departments to prevent him doing as he wished.

In the days of the Queen's grandfather and great-grandfather, George V and Edward VII, Sandringham had been run on grand lines as a country estate dedicated to regal pleasures. Edward VIII, even before he became King, regarded the place as an expensive white elephant and during his brief reign it was allowed to run down somewhat. George VI had done something to change this, but wartime economy still showed. Philip saw no reason why the place should not be made to pay its way or even turn a profit.

As always, he started off by exploring and questioning, driving around in a Land Rover, plodding about in gum boots. The wife of an estate worker, answering a knock at the door of her cottage one morning, almost fainted when she saw the Consort on the doorstep. Could he come in and take a look at repairs recently carried out to the place?

Philip wanted to know what everyone did and how they did it. 'The Duke's naval inspections,' estate workers christened his visits. Not without cause. His navy-neat mind was quick to spot anything that was not tidily shipshape and precisely Bristol fashion. Like the wood shavings which littered the floor of the carpenters' shop. 'Surely one of you could spare time to sweep this place out.' Nor was he enthused by the practice of stacking ice for the cold store on the floor of the yard and he gave instructions for wooden pallets to be fashioned so that the ice could be stored clear of the ground.

But these were small, almost trivial things. More important was the fact that he made suggestions which were to result, over a period of time, in Sandringham being transformed from a slightly run-down pleasure estate into a viable commercial proposition. Mushrooms instead of orchids were planted in one of the vast greenhouses. A pig farm was started on commercial Scandinavian lines. The pigs went for packaged bacon. Milk was sold to the local Co-op. Peas went for freezing and fruit for canning and jam-making. With an eye to the future, more timber – oak, poplar, spruce and pine – was planted. Later, and similarly, at Windsor, disused acres were persuaded to sprout vegetables and derelict bullock houses became the pecking ground for free-range hens.

It was, therefore, not all defeat and more events occurred to lift his initial cloud of depression. Home life, if less free and easy than it had been in pre-monarchy days, was nevertheless happy, even if he continued to feel that Bobo MacDonald exercised too much influence. He was still fond of practical jokes, though these now involved the children rather than the Queen. Jumping beans, squeaking fruit and a fearful toy spider, brought home by Papa, enlivened nursery life. He began teaching Charles to swim in the palace pool. There was the always cheerful comradeship of Mike Parker and the polo field as an outlet for frustration. There was wildfowling with James Robertson Justice and convivial evenings at the home of Uffa Fox with the fun of bellowing singsongs round the piano and hiding a 'raspberry' cushion for some unsuspecting victim to sit on.

But if Philip enjoyed the occasional evening spent at Uffa Fox's home at Cowes, he did not always get the same pleasure from his actual sailing, whether at Cowes or elsewhere. So many sight-seeing pleasure boats surrounded him when he raced at Cowes in coronation year that he was forced to alter course on more than one occasion, giving vent to his feelings with a characteristic succession of expletives. He had the same problem, this time in the form of a fishing boat laden with sightseers, when he took part in the Clyde Fortnight. Mike Parker did his best to make things easier for Philip when more pleasure craft took off in pursuit of the royal yachtsman the following day. 'The Duke's had enough,' he bawled at them through a loud-hailer. 'Give the man a chance.'

For this reason, and others, Philip seldom derived real enjoyment from his sailing. There was to be trouble later over *Fairey Fox*, the 24-foot half-decker which Uffa Fox designed for him. At Cowes, in a race for 19–30 foot yachts, he won on handicap. The following day he won the Vanity Challenge Cup for cruising yachts. Philip had won 'by proven skill and sailing ability,' said the Commodore of the Royal Yacht Squadron, but there were complaints from other yachtsmen that the handicapping had been unfair. Such taunts stung and Philip was never to race *Fairey Fox* again officially.

But if sailing left much to be desired, flying was not only totally enjoyable but also represented another triumph over what Philip, in a much later speech, was to refer to as 'The dead hand of the No-men'. When members of a flying club, in the days when Philip was first flapping his wings, complained of being grounded so that he could practice in safety – a veto, incidentally, of which he knew nothing – one of his aides sent them a letter saying, 'If you think you have difficulties getting into the air, they are nothing to what he has to go through.'

There were objections from 'Their Airships', as Philip categorised the top brass, all along the line. Winston Churchill, the Secretary of State for Air and the AOC Home Command all raised opposition of one sort or another. But Philip persisted and it was finally agreed that he could learn to fly. But there were to be no aerobatics, he was warned, and no night flying. He began his flying lessons on a Chipmunk at RAF station White Waltham in November, 1952, with Flight Lieutenant Caryl Gordon from the Central Flying School as his instructor. Mike Parker somehow managed to get in on the act and learned to fly at the same time. Philip went solo the following month after ten hours and graduated, in turn, to a Harvard, an Oxford, a Devon and a Heron of the Queen's Flight. Each step forward represented a fresh battle with 'Their Airships' fought and won. Even the comparatively small matter of moving on from a Harvard to an Oxford had to be referred to the Chief of Air Staff, who referred it in turn to the prime minister, before Philip was free to go ahead. He was presented with his 'wings' by the Chief of Air Staff in a small ceremony at Buckingham Palace in the May of coronation year.

More than anyone, Philip has been responsible, at least as far as royal travel is concerned, for bringing the Monarchy out of the horse-and-buggy era into the jet age. But for him it would have been many more years before royal tours moved beyond the ship and train concept of travel, still in vogue when the Queen undertook her post-coronation Commonwealth tour.

In one form or another, the battle between Philip and 'Their Airships' went on for years. His desire to fly jets resulted in more opposition from Churchill. But Philip was learning to stand up to opposition and he went on to fly Meteors and Vampires. There was another battle over helicopters, regarded in those days as far too dangerous for royal travel. Once let him start piloting one of those and the next thing you knew he'd be taking the Queen up with him. The mere thought nearly produced a rash of heart failure among 'Their Airships'! But being forbidden to fly helicopters did not mean that he could not use them. As early as the Whitsun of coronation year a Royal Navy chopper touched down on the hallowed lawn of Buckingham Palace and Philip climbed aboard, on his way to visit Commonwealth troops arriving in Britain for the coronation ceremony. Elizabeth watched the take-off and waited apprehensively for his return around lunchtime. Everything went smoothly – until Churchill heard about it later and protested vehemently.

In time Philip overcame the official opposition to helicopters. In 1956 he was allowed to take a helicopter conversion course, one result of which was a take-off from the palace lawn and a touchdown on the flight deck of the Australian aircraft carrier *Melbourne* in Portsmouth harbour. He obtained his private pilot's licence in 1959 and when the Queen's Flight was re-equipped with Andovers he did a conversion course on them, too. Over the years he has guested at the controls of such varied aircraft as Boeings, Viscounts, Comets, Tridents, Constellations, Hovercraft (which may or may not rank as an aircraft) and even Concorde.

Philip had no cause to complain of any lack of work in coronation year. He served as chairman of the Coronation Commission (even if the bulk of the real graft was done by the Duke of Norfolk, in his capacity as Earl Marshal of England, and his staff). He helped to select the designs for the new stampage and coinage. He came up with the idea for lighting the lumbering four-ton state coach used for the coronation procession by installing batteries under the seats. Despite sharing most of his wife's coronation programme, seventy-six major engagements squeezed into thirty days of celebration, he somehow managed to find time to play in more than twenty polo games and his participation was to account for much of the sport's subsequent popularity, particularly from 1955 on when he had his own ground laid out at Smith's Lawn, Windsor. With television cameras turning it into a spectator sport for the masses, Smith's Lawn quickly found itself having to cope with record crowds of over 15,000.

With his wife taking the leading role, he took part in a rehearsal for the coronation ceremony. His part required him to kneel before her, take the Oath of Fealty, rise, kiss her cheek, touch the crown and back away. All sound tradition no doubt, but anachronistic and at rehearsal Philip took it perhaps a shade too lightheartedly. Or so Elizabeth appears to have thought. Sternly she called him back and had him do it over again.

But no one could say that he lacked dignity or seriousness on the actual day of coronation. Indeed, he entered into things with such enthusiasm that he dislodged the massive crown somewhat and the Queen had to readjust it.

On her wedding day Elizabeth, by her own wish, had taken the full bridal vow to obey and serve him as well as love and honour him. On coronation day the situation was reversed with Philip kneeling to her and taking the ancient oath: 'I Philip, Duke of Edinburgh, do become your liege man of life and limb and of earthly worship; and faith and truth will I bear unto you, to live and die, against all manner of folks. So help me God.'

Fatherhood (1)

If some people had sneered at *Magpie*, during the short spell Philip was in command, as 'Edinburgh's private yacht', others were equally quick to label the Queen's new yacht 'Philip's Folly'. Both as a naval man and the Queen's husband, it was natural enough that Philip should be enthusiastic that a new royal yacht was being built to replace the old *Victoria & Albert*, if only because the ship was no longer particularly seaworthy, and never really had been. It had been built over fifty years earlier from plans borrowed from the Tsar of Russia and some confusion between metric and imperial measurements had meant that it was never very stable from the start. But to blame Philip for the £2.1 million cost of building the new royal yacht was not only unfair on the man, but crediting him with rather more influence and authority than he possessed at the time. *Britannia* had originally been at the blueprint stage as far back as the brief reign of Edward VIII. Three times – because of the Abdication, then the outbreak of the Second World War, then the death of George VI – actual construction had been postponed. Work was finally put in hand soon after Elizabeth succeeded to the throne and *Britannia* was launched in coronation year in fond expectation that the fitting-out would be completed in time for the Commonwealth tour. This would have meant holding state banquets on board at the various ports of call.

As a test case, Philip entrained various royal aides and palace servants to Portsmouth, where a full-scale meal was cooked in the yacht's kitchen and served in the yacht's dining room. If it all sounds rather like another case of youthful high jinks, it did enable Philip to point out that seating accommodation for thirty-two was hardly adequate for a state banquet. As a result, side wings were added to the existing dining table bringing the maximum seating accommodation to fifty-six. Uncle Dickie similarly came up with the idea for an ingenious table runner, electrified so that specially-adapted candelabra could be spiked in anywhere along the table.

After all that, *Britannia* was not ready at the outset of the Commonwealth tour and the Royals had to make do with the liner *Gothic*. Even at sea Philip had to have some sporting activity to fill his leisure time and he was soon busy organising games of seven-a-side deck hockey between ship's officers and the Royal entourage. The way Philip liked to play, it was deck hockey almost without rules and with very few holds barred. As one participant recalls, 'Anything went except downright murderous assault.' Not only were knuckles whacked and shins cracked, but even backs and shoulders sustained bruising blows in the process. And Philip played most aggressively of all. 'You must be mad playing a game like that,' Elizabeth told him at the end of one session.

After each game the two sides cooled off in the ship's pool. On one such occasion Philip noticed that two Royal Marines orderlies who had taken part in the game were missing from among those sporting in the pool. He asked where they were. It was with some degree of embarrassment that he was informed that they were barred from using the pool. After all, they were only sergeants. Philip wasn't about to have that sort of demarcation line aboard any ship he was on. 'Nonsense,' he retorted. 'Of course they can use the pool.'

Philip was also very much in evidence the day *Gothic* crossed the equator, his nose red with greasepaint and a blue-and-white butcher's apron flapping about his legs during the traditional crossing-the-line ceremony. Elizabeth escaped becoming one of her husband's victims on the grounds that she had gone through the ceremony when she journeyed to South Africa with her parents, though she was in fact let off with no more than a genteel powdering even on that occasion. But those who had not previously crossed the line, including Philip's cousin, Lady Pamela Mountbatten found themselves unceremoniously dragged before King Neptune in the person of Detective Inspector Frank Kelley, Philip's security man, tried and found guilty on diverse charges and committed to the untender mercies of the Barber (Mike Parker) and his assistant (Philip). A good deal of whitewash and cochineal went flying in all directions and the proceedings ended with everyone doing their best to throw everyone else into the ship's pool.

If the *Guinness Book of Records* contained a section dealing with royal tours, this 1953–4 Commonwealth Tour would still top the list all these years later. Greater use of air travel has resulted in more mileage being logged on some more recent tours, but it has still to be surpassed for duration. It needed only eight more days for it to have lasted six months. In that time the royal couple travelled 49,000 miles, visited ten countries, attended 135 receptions, fifty balls, banquets and garden parties and shook hands 13,000 times. More reconciled to playing second fiddle in the royal orchestra than he had been a year earlier, Philip was constantly at his wife's side, raising her spirits if ever they flagged – 'Buck up, darling' – helping things along with the breeziness of his own personality, bridging the conversational gap if she dried up (as she sometimes did in those days) and being protective if she needed protecting from the demands of her public.

That he was conscious, however, of his secondary role was shown by the wry comment he made the day a couple were presented to him as 'Dr and Mr Robinson'.

'Why not Mr and Dr Robinson?' queried Philip.

'Because,' Mr Robinson explained, 'in our family my wife is the more important person.'

'Yes, we have that sort of problem in our family too,' replied Philip, grinning.

If Philip was assigned to play second fiddle on official platforms, it was a very different matter at grass-roots level. With the girls, in particular, he was very much sought after. Those responsible for organising the Australian section of the tour were initially puzzled as to why there were always so many girls lining one side of the royal route than the other. Then the answer dawned on them. It was the side Philip always sat in the royal car. And the girls made no secret of the fact that what they felt for him was a good deal more than the combination of awe, hero-worship and admiration normally accorded to royalty. In Sydney they pursued him with a chorus of wolf-whistles. In Hobart they blew kisses. One girl, when it was her turn to be presented to him at an official function, gave him a wink of such come-hitherish suggestiveness that even Philip, for once, was at loss for words.

The legend of the witty Philip grew as the tour progressed. His every remark was twisted and burnished by commentators and reporters to give it a semblance of wit. But some of the gems were his own. When teenage triplets were presented to him in Hastings, New Zealand he commented: 'Ah, I think it's really their mother we should be congratulating.' Meeting a 6-foot 4-inch town clerk at a civic reception in Melbourne: 'Ah, you look like a man who could carry a lot of responsibility.' Retrieving a small toddler who had scrambled on to the royal dais and handing him back to his mother: 'It seems we need nannies instead of security men.'

In Stratford, New Zealand, he stopped to bandy pleasantries with a team of local 'marching girls' in white boots and short, pleated skirts. 'How long have you been marching?' he asked one sixteen-year-old with an array of five medals on her tunic. 'Five years,' she told him.

The girl next to her, hardly any older, was almost covered in medals. 'My goodness,' said Philip, 'you must have been marching an awful long time.'

It was Philip, more than anyone, who introduced the human touch into the tour on both a public and personal level. Maoris in one New Zealand area were delighted when he took the Queen to inspect one of their meeting houses though it was not on the official itinerary. In Tasmania, he arranged for her to spend a night with old friends of his Navy days. In Australia he slipped away on his own one night to visit his old friend, Joe Fallon.

Fallon, who was not expecting him, answered the door in his pyjamas.

There were times, on that tour, when Philip flogged himself into a state of near-exhaustion. Although he had been late at a civic dinner the night before, he climbed out of bed at five o'clock one morning to fly 300 miles to Wellington to attend the mass funeral of the twenty-one unidentified victims of the worst rail disaster in New Zealand history. Then he flew straight back to rejoin the Queen for their official itinerary, snatching some sleep en route.

There were other similar instances where he drove himself beyond the reasonable bounds of royal duty and if, in consequence, his temper snapped occasionally it was hardly surprising. There was one occasion when a crowd gathered outside his hotel late at night chanting 'We want Philip' over and over again. Exhausted, he was in no mood to grin and wave at them. He stalked out of his room in his dressing gown and buttonholed the nearest security man. 'Can't you make those people go away? I have to get some sleep.' Similarly, in what was then Ceylon, where he had a garland of flowers stuffed over his head at one whistle-stop. Back out of sight aboard the royal train, he jerked the flowers angrily from around his neck. 'I hate those bloody things.'

Back home, the royal calendar resumed its traditional form, Windsor for Easter, Balmoral in summer, Sandringham at Christmas. Philip was rapidly extending his work-load. But he was still frustrated. And sometimes bored. So it was a relief to take off for Vancouver to open what were still known as the Empire Games. He tacked on a tour of his own, very different in concept from the Commonwealth tour which he had so recently undertaken with Elizabeth which he considered had been too stiff with protocol. For his own solo tour, he bush-hopped to Whitehorse, Yellowknife, Coppermine, Radium City and Fort Simpson, the old frontier headquarters of the Hudson Bay Company, meeting Indians and Eskimos, mounties, trappers and prospectors, sampling bison, caribou and moose at meal-times. For penetrating the Arctic Circle the Royal Canadian Air Force awarded him the status of 'an airborne iceworm', whatever that was. The certificate went nicely with the one he got in wartime for his coal-trimming slog, anyway.

He was also given a medal for attending the Empire Games. That was the year marathon runner Jim Peters collapsed within sight of the finishing line. Philip, on his return to Britain, had his medal mounted on a stand, inscribed 'For A Most Gallant Marathon Runner' and sent it to Peters.

On trips to Germany to visit British troops he took time out to see something of his sisters and their offspring. Margarita had five children, Theodora four and Sophie eight, by two husbands. Theodora and Sophie were amused on one occasion when he turned up wearing a kilt, having come straight on from reviewing the Cameron Highlanders at Luneburg.

By now, he was well accustomed to wearing a kilt upon occasion. It was part of the 'regulation' royal dress during visits to Balmoral, where on the occasion of the Gillies' Ball, Philip would don full Highland regalia to head the opening grand march with Elizabeth. He had become an enthusiastic dancer and a Paul Jones invariably found him in full throttle. 'Why don't you lot dance more?' he yelled at a group of more bashful males on one occasion as he swept past them in partnership with one of the Balmoral housemaids.

As a member of the Royal Family, he has a choice of three tartans, Royal Stewart, Hunting Stewart and the Balmoral tartan designed by that earlier royal consort, Prince Albert.

Hanging like a shadow over monarchy at this time was the problem of Princess Margaret's attachment to Peter Townsend. For the Queen, it was as much a personal family problem as a constitutional one and, as such, she could discuss it freely with Philip. It would have been ridiculous for her not to have done so. Townsend was already equerry to George VI when Philip first went to Balmoral back in 1946, so the two men knew each other well. Though both had distinguished war records – Townsend, a wartime fighter ace, had eleven enemy 'kills' to his credit – there the similarity ended. Philip was essentially a man's man; Townsend more of a ladies' man. At Sandringham and Balmoral he did not take part in the shooting excursions, but would turn up later with the ladies to watch, laughing and chatting with Margaret, sometimes to Philip's irritation. 'Can't you two keep quiet,' he snapped at them on one occasion.

Philip had no say in the decision to 'exile' Townsend to Brussels. Nor, for matter of that, did Elizabeth. What she did was done on the advice of Churchill and the old guard of royal aides inherited from her father. But Philip disliked the whole business immensely. It 'diminished the dignity of the Crown,' he said, and he made his feelings plain when Margaret spent a weekend at Windsor with him and the Queen shortly after Townsend's return to Britain. The three of them had a long heart-to-heart talk over dinner that weekend which ended with Margaret in tears. Just over a week later she issued her statement of renunciation.

In 1955 Philip and Uncle Dickie flew together to Germany to help Philip's mother (who was also Dickie's sister) celebrate her seventieth birthday. A month later Philip was in Germany again, at Langenburg, for Margarita's silver wedding. From time to time he had his older German nephews, Margarita's son Kraft and Theodora's two, Max and Lüdwig, to Balmoral for shooting holidays. With war-time scars not yet fully healed, such visits were kept as low-key as possible.

Philip tried to maintain a similarly low profile when two of his nieces, Sophie's daughter Christina and Margarita's daughter Beatrix, came to London to study in 1956. He rented an apartment for them in the luxury Dolphin Square complex in the name of his Treasurer, 'Boy' Browning. But the secret leaked out, rumours started, there were critical newspaper headlines and the girls were accorded a somewhat chilly reception in some quarters.

About this time Philip helped the Queen in re-planning their private apartment at Windsor Castle. The old oak-panelled dining room, dark and sombre, was transformed into a light, bright sitting room while King George VI's old sitting room became the new dining room. Bedroom and bathroom were completely modernised. On his 1954 trip to the Yukon Philip had seen hotel rooms in which divans became beds at night and writing desks did duty also as dressing tables. Elizabeth liked the idea when he explained it to her and it was introduced into the rooms of the new guest wing.

Philip was not a man to summon servants when he wanted something done. He would set to and do it himself. So when the idea of re-positioning the furniture in the Green Drawing Room came to him one weekend, he simply moved it around. However, he returned the following weekend to find it had all been restored to its original position. So he moved it again and this time it stayed put.

Something else Philip had brought back from Canada provided a lot of fun during family holidays at Balmoral – a portable barbecue outfit, a gadget rarely seen in Britain at that time. Philip would personally go along to the kitchen to select the steaks, chops and sausages and he would do the cooking while the Queen and Anne mixed batter for pancakes. On a subsequent visit to Canada in 1957 he was quick to spot a yet more elaborate barbecue outfit, complete with rotary spit, and promptly sent one of his aides out to buy it. Barbecuing was done in the open air, of course, but Philip, who rather fancied himself as a cook at this time, also imported an electric frying-pan into the Royals' private dining room at the palace so that he could cook his own bacon, sausage and eggs at breakfast time. Unfortunately, the smell of fried food not only permeated into the other rooms of the apartment but tended to linger on for most of the day. The Queen's sitting room-study, which is right next door to the dining room, was particularly affected. She stood it for some time before remarking upon it, after which Philip's frying pan vanished as quickly as it had appeared.

To his children, he was an ideal father – very much a fun father. 'He was marvellous with them,' their nanny, Mabel Anderson, was to recall later. 'He always set aside time to read to them or put together little model toys.' He built sandcastles with them on the beach at Holkham. He would join them in games of football in the motorway-wide corridors at Windsor and play cowboys and Indians with them in the shrubberies. One hot summer's day, before Windsor had its own swimming pool, he not only encouraged them to take a dip in the fountain but put on swimming trunks and joined them. At Balmoral he took them on camping adventures, loading them into a Land Rover, along with sleeping bags and cooking equipment, to spend the day swimming, fishing and sailing and the night in a loch-side cabin. At Sandringham, over Christmas, he organised exciting treasure hunts and showed them how to build snowmen. He emerged from the house there one snowy winter's day to find young Charles throwing snowballs at a patrolling policeman. 'Don't just stand there, man,' he called out, cheerfully. 'Bung some back.'

Philip taught Anne, as well as Charles, to swim in the palace pool. He also taught Charles to sail, fish and aim a gun. He had a miniature polo mallet made for the boy so that they could play bicycle polo together. He took Charles with him to Hickling Broad on a coot-shooting expedition. Philip did the actual shooting, of course, while Charles helped to retrieve the dead birds with an angler's net. The two of them spent the night at a local pub, *The Pleasure Boat Inn*.

But he could be a firm father, too, when the occasion required. He once gave Charles a sound spanking for pulling faces at people from a window. Anne came in for a similar spanking when she staged a display of tantrums aboard the royal yacht on one occasion.

He was a concerned father, and was not completely happy at this stage with the way in which his son, at least, was being brought up. He knew from his own experience what it was like for a young male to be raised in a house filled mainly with women and now he saw the same thing happening all over again with Charles. Except for Philip, who was often away, the boy was surrounded on all sides by petticoats; those of his mother, sister, nanny and governess. Philip, at least, had had to rough it a bit in childhood. Charles didn't even have that to offset the cottonwool nature of his upbringing. Almost everything was done for him. He didn't even have to bother to close a door behind him as a footman would rush to do that for him. This infuriated Philip as much as it had done when footmen rushed to open doors for him. 'Leave it alone, man,' he would call. 'Let him do it himself. Call him back.'

Boarding school, Philip thought, would soon put that right. Elizabeth was not so sure. She favoured the idea of a private tutor, but eventually Philip talked her round.

Rift?

A happy marriage is hardly the stuff of which headlines are made. But a split between Queen and Consort . . . now that could be almost guaranteed to boost circulation. Lacking reality, many European publications have never been slow to fabricate fights, splits, rifts between Philip and his royal wife, even imminent divorce. The French have been particularly good at it. During the first fourteen years of royal marriage, the couple were, according to various French publications, on the brink of divorce on no fewer than seventy-three occasions. No one outside the avid readers of such publications, and not all of them, take such stories seriously. But the 'Royal Rift' headlines of 1957 were something else. They started in America, not France, and were taken so seriously that in a matter of days they had circumnavigated the world. So how much truth was there in it all?

It started with Philip going through one of his spells of disenchantment with royal routine. If he was no longer so depressed as he had been at the outset of his wife's reign, he had not yet adapted sufficiently to be entirely free of boredom and frustration. And if he did not have the sort of mistress some of the more sensational newspaper stories tried to pin on him later, there was an old mistress he still hankered after at times – the sea. An invitation to host the 1956 Olympic Games in Melbourne offered both a relief from boredom and a chance to get back to the sea again. Just as he had made the 1954 Empire Games in Vancouver the focal point for a pioneering royal tour of the Canadian Arctic, so he now began scheming how Melbourne might be turned into a similar focal point for a royal Antarctic expedition. He could

[116]

pop ashore to visit survey teams in the Falkland Isles. Drop in on the Trans-Antarctic Expedition. He even toyed briefly with the idea of sailing the royal yacht into the Ross Sea, but decided against this. By the time he had everything organised what had originally been envisaged as a quick out-and-back trip by air had become a sea-going adventure which was to last for four months. It started on 13 October when he flew out to Mombasa where *Britannia* was waiting for its royal Admiral of the Fleet to come aboard. His wife and his sister Sophie were at the airport to see him off.

The invitation to the Melbourne Olympics also triggered off another idea in Philip's ever-fertile brain. His old headmaster, Kurt Hahn, had long wanted to promote Gordonstoun's 'More is in you' outlook on a wider basis; to see other youngsters given the same character-building opportunities he was giving the boys who passed through his own hands. In a small way, in fact, he had already done something about it. The Moray Badge which he instituted at Gordonstoun as an incentive for endeavour was open to boys of the surrounding district as well as the school. But Hahn was not content with that. He wanted to see his Moray Badge scheme, or something similar, go national and, being Hahn, was quite prepared to badger his most famous pupil into doing something about it. Philip, at first, was reluctant to get involved. He was not sure that it was the sort of thing that would go down well in Britain and the outburst which greeted a speech in which he advocated the character-building qualities of National Service had tended to reinforce that view. But now he saw how the thing might be made to work. Give the kids a chance to go for gold, Olympic style. So the Duke of Edinburgh's Award scheme, with its gold, silver and bronze awards, came into being.

The beginnings of the scheme, that first year, were relatively modest. Some seven thousand boys were persuaded, cajoled or coerced into taking part and slightly more than one thousand emerged at the other end with silver and bronze medals. Philip, in launching the Scheme, described it in the official handbook as 'an introduction to leisure time activities, a challenge to the individual to personal achievement'. The second year saw over

8,500 new entrants willing, even eager, to participate and the number of award winners rose to 2,584, including the first golds – eighty-two of them. The next year saw girls as well as boys entering and Commonwealth countries were clamouring to get in on the act. Suddenly the whole scheme took off – there were about 60,000 new entrants a year in the 1960s and up to 90,000 a year in the 1970s. By the time Philip's Award scheme celebrated its coming-of-age in 1978, over a million and a quarter British youngsters had been stamped with its character-building imprint. Outside Britain, a further 250,000 children in thirty-three other countries, from Canada to the Cayman Islands, from Australia to Jamaica and New Zealand to Bermuda, had also participated. Not all the Commonwealth countries which borrowed Philip's scheme linked it with his ducal title. In the Seychelles it became simply the Youth Award, in Kenya and Sierra Leone the President's Award, in Ghana the Head of State Award and in Lesotho the Prince Mohato Award. But such changes of name did not alter the fact that it is the same scheme which Hahn dreamed up and his most famous pupil brought to fruition. 'It has probably done more for people than anything else I have been involved in,' Philip says, diffidently. It is also, perhaps, the one thing for which he will be remembered when all else is forgotten.

What with planning the Award scheme and blue-printing plans for his Antarctic expedition, Philip was kept busy. He wanted no undue ceremony on his forthcoming trip, he told his aides. To his mind, there had been a deal too much of that on the round-the-world tour he had undertaken with Elizabeth in the aftermath of her coronation. 'Too many displays, speeches and guards of honour,' he objected when shown the proposed itinerary for part of the trip. Of course pomp and ceremony could not be entirely eliminated, however much Philip may have wished it, but, as in Canada in 1954, they were kept to a minimum. In Australia, in particular, he managed to get sufficiently far off the normal beaten royal track to visit an outback cattle station and the town called Alice, to meet and talk with the hydro-electric roustabouts in the Snowy Mountains and the uranium miners of

Rum Jungle. One night in Darwin, after an official reception at Government House, he traded his tuxedo for a bush jacket and went hunting crocodiles, bagging a six-footer.

On such informal excursions, that kindred spirit, Mike Parker, was his invariable companion. There was another crocodile-hunting excursion among the mangrove swamps of the Gambia river. On that occasion, they encountered an unusually large specimen and both hammered shots into it. Then Parker went over the side of their boat to secure it with a rope. He would have been a shade less eager perhaps had it dawned on him that the creature might not be dead. Hauled up and lashed to the side, it proceeded to lash out so violently with its tail that it inflicted considerable damage to the boat before it was despatched with a knife.

Although it had not been planned that way, the expedition also took on something of the flavour of a sentimental journey. In Mombasa, right at the outset, Philip ran across an old friend of his Gordonstoun days, James Orr, at that time a chief inspector in the Kenyan police. Later, when Mike Parker was to blame himself for much of the dirt flung at Philip and insist upon tendering his resignation, Philip, unable to get Parker to change his mind, contacted Orr again and invited him to take over as his private secretary. In Colombo he ran across the beat-up little car he had once bought for 450 rupees, half down, the rest by instalments in those impecunious wartime days. 'Hope the brakes are better than when I had her,' he joked. Going ashore on Tristan da Cunha, he found that his old command, *Magpie*, had been there not long before and had left an ensign behind as a souvenir of her visit.

In the light of later events two small incidents take on special significance. From Australia, on 20 November he put in a radio-telephone call to Britain to let Elizabeth know he had not forgotten it was their ninth wedding anniversary. And in New Zealand he spotted a picture adorning the wall of an hotel, asked if he could have it and took it away with him to hang in his cabin aboard *Britannia*. It was a reproduction of a painting of Elizabeth done by Edward Halliday.

As the royal yacht headed for the Antarctic, news bulletins specially prepared by the BBC and transmitted by the Admiralty twice daily kept Philip and others on board in touch with what was going on back home in Britain and the world at large. Radio-telephone calls to his wife kept him posted on family affairs. Such calls were timed as far as possible to reach Elizabeth at Windsor around lunchtime on Sundays, but the timing was sometimes unpredictable and a call came through one Sunday while she was in church. However, it was known that she would be calling at Royal Lodge to see her mother when she came out of church and the call was transferred there. With the approach of Christmas Philip's calls were routed to Sandringham instead. And among the gift-wrapped packages he opened aboard the yacht on Christmas Day was a tape recording on which he heard his wife and children wishing him 'A happy Christmas' while the snappy little royal corgis yapped excitedly in the background . . . another small incident which takes on special significance ahead of the coming storm.

With the bottom almost falling out of the thermometer aboard *Britannia*, permission was given for beards to be worn. More than that, a contest was organised with prizes of razor blades and after-shave for the bushiest, gaudiest, most distinguished and least successful efforts. Philip himself did not enter the contest though he grew a beard with russet overtones.

He had brought his cameras along and took photographs of albatross, skua gulls, penguins – the start of a photographic collection which was eventually to become a book, *Birds From Britannia*. He also made his first attempt at oil painting under the tuition of artist Edward Seago, turning out seascapes and landscapes as well as trying his hand at portraiture. With Seago's help, he designed and produced his own version of the 'airborne iceworm' certificate he had been given in the Canadian Arctic two years before. As a result, those aboard *Britannia* the day it penetrated the Antarctic found themselves members of the very un-royal Order of the Red Nose.

His thirst for knowledge was as strong as ever. Coming across a whaling ship, nothing would prevent him from going aboard to watch what was going on even though transfer from royal yacht to whaler involved a trip in a wicker basket. His return was not welcomed. 'The stench clung to us for days,' recalls a man who was aboard *Britannia* at the time. Curiously, it is the smells rather than the sights which linger in the memories of those who accompanied Philip. 'The whaler, the penguin rookeries, the elephant seals – they all stank.'

At Loubert, just north of the Antarctic Circle, with Mike Parker, Sir Raymond Priestley and an American meteorologist from Base W making up a men's four, Philip slipped and skidded his way through an impromptu tennis game on ice. Reaching the Falkland Isles, he managed to visit seven of the eleven survey teams located there at the time. On Deception Island the walls of the mess were decorated with lengths of necktie snipped from previous visitors. Philip not only volunteered to sacrifice his own necktie to augment the collection, but instructed his entourage to do the same. Parker, however, was not wearing a necktie. So they simply yanked out the tail of his tartan shirt and snipped a bit off that instead. Afterwards Philip entertained the survey team to dinner aboard *Britannia*. The meal was followed by a film show in the yacht's dining room. The film they saw that evening was *Seven Brides For Seven Brothers*, perhaps, as Philip joked afterwards, 'not such a good idea' as entertainment for men who had not seen a woman in months.

Back home in Britain, as Philip's offbeat expedition neared its end, his own long separation from Elizabeth proved to be not such a good idea. Were people in Britain really 'talking openly of a rift between Queen Elizabeth and the Duke of Edinburgh', as a story cabled to the *Baltimore Sun* suggested? Well, maybe one or two people on the fringe of the café society cocktail circuit in London were enjoying a spot of gossip, but in the industrial and agricultural heartland of the nation they had better things to talk about. And maybe even the know-it-alls were confusing Philip and Elizabeth with Mike and Eileen Parker, who had reached the end of the matrimonial road and had decided to separate. 'If you are a foreign correspondent, it is your duty to report rumours. I was most careful to point out that they were just rumours,' the

Baltimore Sun's London correspondent, Joan Graham, defended herself when the storm broke. But by that time the story had been picked up, repeated, garnished, enlarged and further developed by other newspapers throughout America, in Canada, Australia, France of course, Germany and elsewhere. Reporters from all parts of the world descended on London with instructions to dig up the royal dirt. No likely stone was left unturned; anything and everything was seized upon to bolster and colour the royal rift rumour. What about Philip and the Thursday Club? For all that it was ages since he had been to one of its functions. Was it really just an innocent literary luncheon club? What about his visits to the studio apartment of court photographer Baron? Baron, however, had been dead for some months. At Buckingham Palace, the then press officer, Richard Colville, found himself on the receiving end of some of the most pointed questions he had ever been asked. Not that even the most investigative newspaperman was likely to get any change from a press officer who had once declined to reveal the colour of Prince Charles' eyes on the grounds that this was getting 'too personal'. 'It is quite untrue that there is any rift between the Queen and the Duke of Edinburgh,' Colville snapped.

So plain a denial hardly satisfied foreign newsmen sent to London at such considerable expense. They frequented the bars and eating places of Fleet Street offering dollars, marks and francs galore for the 'low-down' on the alleged royal rift. Finding no takers, they fell back on less reliable sources of information and the stories continued. There was mention of 'an actress', 'a singer' and a 'London party girl', of 'unnamed' women and 'mystery' women. Parker's resignation, which he tendered when the yacht reached Gibraltar in the aftermath of his wife's announcement that the two of them had separated, was equally seized upon as the root cause of royal disagreement. The Queen was insisting that Parker should resign, said the stories, while Philip was fighting to retain his old friend and shipmate. In fact, neither Philip nor the Queen wanted Parker to leave and both urged him to withdraw his resignation, Philip on the spot in Gibraltar and the Queen in a personal radio-telephone call to

Parker from London. But Parker, in Philip's words, 'felt he had to go'. Philip drove him to the airport to catch a plane home and accorded him a farewell handshake for all the world to see. Not that it was a final farewell. They were to see each other from time to time in the future.

As at the time of the abdication, Britain's newspapers diplomatically refrained from echoing what was being published overseas until they could do so no longer. And when they did finally run the story, they either kept their distance from it with headlines like QUEEN AND REPORTS ABROAD or denied it – PALACE RUMOURS UNTRUE. But at least one headline urged the absent Consort: FLY HOME PHILIP.

Philip, however, did not fly home. Had he done so, the royal rift rumours might have died an earlier death. With a royal visit to nearby Portugal coming up shortly after, he might equally have exposed himself to the criticism that he was wasting public money. He had been down that road before. Elizabeth was extremely upset by what she read in the newspapers. 'How can they say such cruel things about us?' she asked Bobo Mac-Donald. Philip was angry rather than hurt and a stubborn determination not to be pushed around by the newspapers was perhaps part of the reason he did not change his plans. The decision not to change their original plans was taken in the course of yet another radio-telephone call between Queen and Consort. So Philip stayed on Gibraltar while *Britannia* was scoured of Antarctic grime and restored to the pristine condition essential for the Portuguese state visit.

Philip was clean shaven when he boarded the Viscount jet on which the Queen had flown out to Portugal only to find himself confronted by an array of bushily-bearded faces. This time it was Elizabeth's turn to be the practical joker of the family. She donned a false beard for the moment of reunion and made the members of her entourage do the same. If the 150 newsmen and photographers drawn to Portugal in the hope of witnessing a royal reunion knew nothing of all this merriment, they could still report that all was well with the royal marriage. Elizabeth wore a beaming smile as she and Philip left the aircraft and one sharp-eyed newsman claimed to have spotted 'a smudge of lipstick' on Philip's mouth.

It was not in Philip's nature to stay silent about all that had happened and a welcome-home luncheon at London's Mansion House gave him the opportunity to get things off his chest. 'For most of my life,' he told the other luncheon guests, 'to be away four months from home meant nothing to me. This time, for obvious reasons, it meant much more. But I believe there are some things for which it is worthwhile making some personal sacrifice. I believe the Commonwealth is one of those things and I, for one, am prepared to sacrifice a good deal if, by doing so, I can advance its wellbeing by even a small degree.' He explained away his stopover at Gibraltar by saying that the trip (which, incidentally, cost him £8,000 out of his own pocket) had been completed against every expectation to the day of their original estimate. Ross Sea or not, it was the sort of trip on which anything could have happened, so it was not unreasonable that a contingency time-lag should have been built in. In the event, it proved to be unnecessary. The trip was completed on schedule, which was, said Philip, in a dig at the newspapers, perhaps rather unfortunate as things turned out.

By the time he made that speech he was again a Prince in fact as well as in popular esteem. Only twenty-four hours after they returned from Portugal together, Elizabeth had shown what she thought of the newspaper stories by remedying her father's inadvertent omission at the time he made Philip a Royal Highness. She was pleased, she announced, 'to give and grant unto His Royal Highness the Duke of Edinburgh the style and titular dignity of Prince of the United Kingdom.'

Wind Of Change

Angry though the royal rift furore made Philip while it lasted, distressing though it was to Elizabeth, good resulted from it. It was as though both of them came to see their respective roles and their relationship to each other in a new light. It didn't happen all at once, of course; it was a gradual process, but it was immediately following the royal rift rumours that the beginnings of change were detectable. As though conscious of the fact that her devotion to Monarchy had thrust Philip for too long into a back seat, Elizabeth was more willing to listen to his views. Certainly in family matters and perhaps in other directions also. For while Philip may have been – and still is – barred from seeing the contents of the Boxes and sitting in on his wife's official Audiences with the prime minister and other advisers, it is ridiculous to suppose that conversations over breakfast or of an evening between a wife and husband who are also Queen and Consort are confined entirely to trivialities. For the first time since his wife ascended the throne, Philip's feet were planted firmly enough under the royal dining table for him to begin his self-appointed task of updating the Monarchy, of dragging it, creaking and protesting, out of the Victorian age and into the coming microchip age of the twentieth century.

Philip's case was helped, even if it did not seem that way at the time, by a trenchant article written by the then Lord Altrincham (who later reverted to the more democratic name of John Grigg) in the *National & English Review*. 'The Monarchy will not survive, let alone thrive,' wrote Altrincham-Grigg, 'unless its leading figures exert themselves to the full and with all the imagination that they and their advisers can command.' Elizabeth had always exerted herself to the full, though perhaps, at times, in the wrong direction. Certainly neither she nor her advisers were over-gifted with imagination. Philip was, but until now that had hardly helped. The article went on to detail what Altrincham thought was wrong. Royal presentation parties he saw as 'a grotesque survival'. The Court had 'lamentably failed to move with the times' and its make-up emphasised 'social lop-sidedness'. The Queen's advisers were 'almost without exception people of the tweedy sort'. Her own personality was 'that of a priggish schoolgirl' and her style of speaking 'frankly, a pain in the neck'.

The article brought some loyal Britons close to the verge of apoplexy. Its author should be 'hanged, drawn and quartered', wrote the Duke of Argyll. Someone else tried to put something of this nature into practice and poor Altrincham-Grigg was practically mugged in the street. Although they were phrased in rather purple prose, however, the man's criticisms were not so far removed from Philip's own thinking.

'Will she (the Queen),' Altrincham-Grigg wanted to know, 'have the wisdom to give her children an education very different from her own? Will she, above all, see to it that Prince Charles is equipped with all the knowledge he can absorb without injury to his health and that he mixes during his formative years with children who will one day be bus drivers, dockers, engineers and not merely with future landowners or stockbrokers?'

That was pushing it a bit too far, perhaps. The nearest Charles was to come to mixing with future bus-drivers and dockers was at Trinity College, years later, when he became friendly with a young left-winger who had worked on the buses (and played in a pop group) while waiting for a university place. But the decision that Charles should go to school instead of being educated in isolation by a succession of tutors had, in fact, already been taken at the time the article was published and the process of toughening up the boy in readiness for school had already begun. The dancing lessons he shared with Anne came to an abrupt end. Music lessons were curtailed. Instead of dancing and music, he was sent to a private gym for physical training, to a running track for juvenile athletics and to a sports ground to experience the hard knocks of schoolboy football. Elizabeth, though she gave way to Philip over sending the boy to school, was not entirely happy about it all. She saw possible dangers: he would be stalked by photographers or mobbed by sightseers. Much of which was to happen. Philip was more optimistic. 'I think people will have enough sense to give the boy a break.' As Consort, Philip saw that Charles, as heir to the throne, needed a broader outlook and wider experience than was possible within the cottonwool confines of Buckingham Palace; boarding school was as good a start as any. As a father, he wanted his only son (at that time) to be moulded in his own image, and how better to achieve that than by sending him to the same schools which had moulded him in boyhood.

With hindsight, different schools would perhaps have been better. Charles, in those days, was not the sort of child Philip had been in schooldays. Sending him to schools where Philip had covered himself with so much schoolboy glory meant forcing him to live in his father's giant shadow. He was homesick at Cheam and was never happy at Gordonstoun. The benefits came later, at school in Australia and at Cambridge university.

About the same time that Charles was struggling to find his feet at boarding school, his mother, with Philip's help, was waging her own battle to rid herself of the 'priggish schoolgirl' personality and 'pain in the neck' articulation. Philip himself had long used a tape-recorder in the preparation of his public speeches, standing at a lectern in his study (so that the speech was 'delivered' instead of merely read out) with the tape machine running and then listening to the playback to hear how it sounded. Now he encouraged Elizabeth to employ much the same technique. He also encouraged her to re-think her ideas about appearing on television, which he saw as an important image-maker in the new royal age which lay ahead. He had already appeared on television twice himself, giving a witty account of his Antarctic expedition in a programme entitled *Round The World In Forty Minutes* and acting as link-man for

The Restless Sphere, a 75-minute programme which marked the opening of the Geophysical Year. In an era when television was less hidebound by its own scheduling, his *Round The World* show actually ran to 55 minutes without anyone having the nerve to cut him off. 'Overtime as usual,' he quipped at the end.

Elizabeth, however, was apprehensive of this (to her) new medium. The previous year she had flatly rejected a suggestion that her traditional Christmas Day broadcast to the Commonwealth should be turned into a telecast. Philip understood her nervousness. Despite the success of his own television appearances, he was still rather less confident in front of the camera than was apparent from the results seen on the screen and it was to be years before he finally succeeded in stopping his hands from trembling. Nevertheless, he saw it as an important adjunct to projecting the royal image and when the Queen was again approached to appear on television during a forthcoming visit to Canada, he not only encouraged her to accept but worked with her to overcome her nerves. A preliminary run-through at Buckingham Palace before leaving for Canada was, frankly, a flop. Another try-out when they reached Canada was better, but not much, and Elizabeth was still nervous and tense as the final few seconds ticked away towards transmission time. Philip, watching her on a monitor screen, decided to jolly her up as he had done so often on public occasions. 'Tell the Queen to remember the wailing and gnashing of teeth,' he said, a cryptic reference to the fact that he had omitted one of the lines of the lesson he had read earlier at an Ottawa church service. His message was passed to Elizabeth just as the red light came on in the studio. She smiled for the first time and was still beaming as the camera tracked in to flash the picture of a happy and radiant Queen into thousands of Canadian homes.

From Canada, the royal couple went on to the United States, visiting Williamsburg (on the 350th anniversary of the first British settlement at nearby Jamestown), Washington and New York. The (at that time) influential and authoritative *Saturday Evening Post* decided to cash in on the visit by publishing a Malcolm Muggeridge article with the provocative catch-line *Does*

Britain Really Need A Queen? Much of what Muggeridge wrote for US consumption was little different from what Altrincham-Grigg had said for British consumption some two months previously, but it went down less well with Philip. 'If they must print such things, does it have to be while we are here?' he demanded, truculently. Perhaps it caught him on a bad day.

It was on one of his good days that he visited the US Institute of Physics and, on leaving the Institute, he decided to take a stroll along Lexington Avenue and 45th Street before dodging through Grand Central Station and along Park Avenue to reach a side entrance of the Waldorf Towers, where he and Elizabeth were staying. But astute New Yorkers, eager to see the Royals, had anticipated the possible use of a side entrance and were clustered around it. Philip shouldered through the throng only to find his way barred by a New York policeman who, momentarily, failed to recognise him. 'It's all right – it's me,' said Philip, grinning.

Back home again in Britain, he continued his efforts to change the anachronistic image of Monarchy, which Altrincham-Grigg saw a failure to move with the times and Muggeridge had described as 'a sort of royal soap opera'. Some of the more soap opera-ish concepts began to disappear and others were toned down. The old presentation parties at Buckingham Palace with their simpering, curtseying debutantes came to an end, to be replaced by extra garden parties encompassing guests from a broader spectrum. Informal luncheon parties to which businessmen, trade unionists, sportsmen, film stars and pop stars were invited, as well as politicians and churchmen, were introduced to enable the Royals to keep more in touch with what was going on outside the Palace. In an era of ever-increasing royal travel, the traditional welcome-back parties at London's Mansion House were curtailed and Elizabeth made it plain that she would no longer attend the same functions year after year. And Altrincham-Grigg was doubtless delighted to find fewer 'people of the tweedy sort' whispering in royal ears at Buckingham Palace as the old guard of royal advisers retired one by one and professionals began taking over. It may not all have been Philip's

9

doing, but he created the atmosphere. Present-day palace servants, in particular, have much for which to thank him. It was due to him that the old attics at the palace, where pages and footmen slept in cubicles they derided as 'horse boxes', were converted into comfortable bedsitters. Thanks to him they no longer had to 'powder' their hair on state occasions, a messy business involving not only soap and water but flour and starch also. 'Ridiculous and unmanly', was Philip's view of this particular piece of pomp and ceremony. They are less likely to thank him, though it seemed a good idea at the time, for lightening the load of gold trim they had previously hauled around on their liveries. Traditionally, royal footmen and pages get to keep their old liveries and all that gold would be worth a fortune at today's bullion prices.

Elizabeth was no more enthused by television than she had been earlier. But having agreed to be televised in Canada, she could hardly refuse a second time when the British Broadcasting Corporation renewed its suggestion that her Christmas Day broadcast should become a telecast. That first Christmas Day telecast was carried out live from Sandringham, in a room converted to an improvised studio for the occasion, with Philip flashing her encouraging grins just out of camera range. For once, Elizabeth managed to avoid the customary 'pain in the neck' royal platitudes of which Altrincham-Grigg had complained, making it clear exactly where she stood in the new permissive age, wagging a remonstrative royal finger at people who 'throw away ageless ideals, would have religion thrown aside, morality in personal and public life made meaningless, honesty counted as foolishness and self-interest set up in the place of self-restraint.' It sounds rather more like Philip than Elizabeth, and perhaps it was.

But if her speech that Christmas Day was an improvement on past platitudes, the same was not true of the television production. Elizabeth, as she has frequently reminded those around her, is 'not a film star' and it all seemed a bit stiff and wooden. It was, however, a start which was to lead in time to the television film *Royal Family* and today's rather less stylised Christmas Day

[130]

broadcasts which Philip refers to irreverently as 'The Queen Show'.

Philip himself was also in the process of change around this time. Though still fond of a laugh and a joke, he was no longer the skylarking young naval officer of yesteryear. Age had something to do with that, of course. But so did the *mystique* of Monarchy with which he found himself so continuously surrounded. Too much pomp and ceremony might still irritate him, but he no longer regarded it quite so irreverently as he had done at the time of the coronation rehearsal. Popular though he was – and is – with the vast majority of his wife's subjects, there were always those lying in wait to criticise him. And sometimes, either from deliberate obstinacy or sheer lack of forethought, it has seemed as though he has manufactured their targets for them. Loyalty to the side, the team spirit, is all very well, but an overdose of it was to result in fresh coals of fire being hurled at him when he escorted Elizabeth on one of their routine royal progresses through Northern England at a time when his Windsor Park polo team was due to play in the final of the Royal Windsor Cup.

In Philip's absence, Peter Barclay was detailed to substitute for him. Then another of the team, Colonel Gerard Leigh, broke a collar-bone. With no other substitute available, a telephone call was put through to Philip. 'Don't worry. I'll be there,' he promised.

To get to Windsor from Holy Island, off the Northumberland coast, which he and Elizabeth were visiting on the day of the game, involved the use of a launch, a destroyer, a fast car, a Heron of the Queen's Flight and another car at the other end. It all seemed a little excessive merely to take part in a polo game and critics of the Consort were not slow to say so. For the record, Philip scored two of his side's seven goals and Windsor Park won the cup.

If he was no longer quite the practical joker he had been in earlier days, Philip was still addicted to gadgets and gimmickry, a fact which was turned to unexpected account the following month. For Elizabeth, it was proving to be a year of rare ill-health. On and off she was ill – with colds, flu, sinus – from January to July. Many royal engagements, public and private, had to be cancelled, including attendance at that year's Cup Final at Wembley. She and Philip were on the royal train, carrying out a tour of Scotland and the North-East, when she awoke one morning with yet another soaring temperature and sore throat. She could hardly speak and Philip, who normally equates other people's coughs and colds with lack of moral fibre, was worried about her. 'You get home and get to bed,' he said. 'I'll handle the rest of this.' While the train carried her south to London, he deputised for her in Carlisle before flying after her. Sinusitus was diagnosed and royal physicians carried out a minor operation to irrigate the affected sinuses. Elizabeth must stay in bed and carry out no more engagements at least until the end of the month, they insisted, a time-lag which took in the Commonwealth Games, being held that year in Cardiff and which she had promised to attend.

Well, if she couldn't go in person, why not let her voice make the trip on its own? Recording technicians brought in equipment rather more sophisticated than Philip's own tape machine and Elizabeth recorded the message she was unable to deliver in person. Philip, going it alone to Cardiff, took the recording with him. The Queen, he told the crowd on the last day of the Games, was 'determined to have some part in this great occasion.' Then, like a magician producing a rabbit from a hat, he conjured up his wife's voice from the ground's amplifying equipment to deliver the news that she was marking the occasion by creating their son, Charles, Prince of Wales.

Fatherhood (2)

Philip has always radiated the sort of masculinity which the opposite sex finds very appealing. Yet he is, perhaps, more of a man's man than a ladies' man, most at home in the all-male atmosphere of a regimental stag party, a ship's bridge in rough weather or the flight deck of an aircraft. So a governmental suggestion in 1959 that he should mount another of his expedition-type royal tours met with an enthusiastic response — once the Treasury had agreed to pay for the trip. His 1957 Antarctic sortie had cost him about £8,000 from his own pocket and he couldn't afford to dig that deep again, he said.

He cut short his Christmas stay at Sandringham to fly out to Delhi and Karachi, where he represented the British Association at two scientific conferences, then joined the royal yacht to sail on to such isolated Commonwealth outposts as the Solomon Islands, the Gilbert and Ellice Islands, and Christmas Island. As always, he proved himself to be an outstanding roving ambassador. And astute. In Hong Kong, where his initial welcome seemed to lack something of the usual enthusiasm, he thought back to a little Chinese girl whom he had occasionally rewarded with chocolate in wartime days as she chipped rust from the hull of *Whelp*. He had her traced and invited to a reception aboard *Britannia*. It was a classic Philip touch and it went down well.

Homeward bound again, he called Elizabeth on 21 April to wish her a happy thirty-third birthday. They had been apart for three months and she drove out to London airport to welcome him back. Such was the enthusiasm of their reunion that when they took off, seven weeks after, for yet another royal tour of

Canada it was in the knowledge that they would shortly become parents all over again. Only they know whether or not this was a deliberate piece of family planning, but Philip, in the course of a public speech, was to say later, 'People want the first child very much. They want the second almost as much. If a third child comes along they accept it as natural, but they haven't gone out of their way to try and get it.'

Either way, Elizabeth was in high spirits when their Comet landed at St John's, Newfoundland, but Philip seemed unusually subdued, owing to concern for his wife's health. A 16,000-mile journey around Canada with some forty-five stops en route, each with its quota of receptions, displays, banquets, public drives and handshakes, was hardly the sort of trip an expectant mother should be undertaking. When he heard of the Queen's condition, Canada's prime minister, John Diefenbaker, suggested that her schedule should be cut. If Philip would happily have gone along with that, Elizabeth herself would not. It was inevitable that the strain should tell and her initial high spirits fade somewhat. The physician travelling with the royal party, Surgeon Captain D. D. Steele-Perkins, had to be called in from time to time. Shrewd newspaper correspondents, to whom the birth of another royal child was almost as great a story as a rumour of possible royal divorce, were quick to put two and two together.

During their trip to Chicago, Elizabeth was looking tense and strained instead of bright and breezy. Philip did his best to cheer things along. 'Relax, darling,' he encouraged her. 'They're mad about you.' But the Liz and Phil enthusiasm with which she was greeted in the American city whose mayor had once offered to bust her grandfather 'on the snoot' could hardly offset the strain of a thirteen-hour day during which she visited the International Trade Fair, the Art Institute and the Museum of Science Industry as well as cramming in a dental appointment to have a lost filling replaced.

As always, concern for his wife made Philip tetchy as the tour ran its course and this tetchiness was reflected in his speeches and conversations alike. He lectured the Canadian Medical Association on the 'state of sub-health' existing in the country and condemned Ontario's liquor laws as 'obsolete and old-fashioned' despite the fact that Britain's own liquor laws were hardly less so. By the time the pair of them reached Whitehorse Elizabeth was so exhausted that Steele-Perkins urged her to take to her bed. Philip added his plea and flew on, alone and worried, to Dawson City. Elizabeth managed to struggle through a further welter of engagements in Edmonton, but was so unwell by that time that the original idea of a leisurely sea trip back to Britain was called off. Instead, the pair of them flew home so that royal physicians could run a thorough check on Elizabeth's condition. A few days' rest worked wonders and Philip was cheered by the news that 'Her Majesty is in the best of health.' To ease the strain on her, he deputised for her at investitures and also flew out to Ghana as substitute for her on a visit she was too advanced in pregnancy to make.

Clerics from Cardinal Wolsey on have always had an important part to play in royal affairs. It was an address by Dr Alfred Blunt, Bishop of Bradford, which first alerted the British public to the imminence of the Abdication. Similarly, it was a sermon by Dr Thomas Bloomer, Bishop of Carlisle, which first raised the question of what name the expected royal baby would bear. As things stood, Dr Bloomer told his congregation, the baby would be born not with the father's name of Mountbatten, but with the mother's name of Windsor. It did not seem right that a child born in wedlock should be deprived of its father's name, a right and privilege enjoyed by every other legitimate child. 'We in this country,' he said, 'have respect for titles, but a family name transcends these and stirs deeper and more powerful emotions in the family circle.' He hoped that the Queen would make it her will and pleasure to secure the same birthright for the new baby that other children enjoyed.

His words struck a responsive chord with Elizabeth. She had long regretted the ease with which she had been swayed, at the outset of her reign, into changing the childrens' name to Windsor and had long wanted to make some fresh sort of change which would be fairer to Philip. 'Her Majesty has had this in mind for a long time and it is close to her heart,' a palace spokesman was to say later. The problem was that she also wished to continue the name of the Royal House established by her grandfather and borne by her father before her.

After discussing the situation with Philip, his Uncle Dickie and Harold Macmillan, her then prime minister, Elizabeth decided upon a compromise solution. The result was a complex and ambiguous royal decree announcing that 'while I and my children shall continue to be styled and known as the House and Family of Windsor, my descendants other than descendants enjoying the style, title or attribute of Royal Highness and the titular dignity of Prince and Princess and female descendants who marry and their descendants shall bear the name of Mountbatten-Windsor'.

What all that meant was anybody's guess at the time. Experts on constitutional law could not agree and one worked it out that the new hyphenated name would apply only to some of Elizabeth's great-grandchildren, which was looking rather a long way into the future. Even Philip, who knew what his wife really intended, was moved to make the wry comment, 'It still makes the children sound like bastards.' What Elizabeth really intended, though this did not become totally clear until Princess Anne married Mark Phillips in the name of Anne Elizabeth Mountbatten-Windsor, spinster, thirteen years later, was that while she herself would still not take her husband's name of Mountbatten, the children, if and when they had need of a surname, would have the new hyphenated name.

Andrew Mountbatten-Windsor was born at Buckingham Palace on 19 February 1960, and irreverent yells of 'Hello, Dad' greeted Philip when he attended the Navy v RAF rugby game at Twickenham the following day. Whether or not he and Elizabeth had 'gone out of their way' to have the new baby, both were delighted, after a gap of ten years, by this opportunity to play mum and dad again.

Early evening found Philip bounding upstairs to the nursery, to spend a few minutes with his second son before the baby was settled down for the night. He was often already dressed for an evening engagement when he visited the nursery and there was one occasion when a second quick change was necessary after his white shirt became smeared with gooey chocolate from Andrew's sticky fingers. Another time, when Andrew was somewhat bigger and the two of them were indulging in a playful bout of fisticuffs, a childish fist found its way through dad's defences. Despite the hurried application of a chunk of raw steak, Philip arrived at a film première later that evening sporting what looked very much like the beginnings of a black eye.

With all three children he was both a fun father and a concerned parent. At Sandringham, that Christmas, he joined Charles and Anne in trying out a new miniature go-kart while insisting that they should wear a safety helmet when using it themselves. He believes in children learning things early. 'Later on there is a sense of embarrassment at being a beginner.' But he also believes in sensible precautions. 'Proper training removes most of the hazards in what, to the uninitiated, look like dangerous activities.' He believes in guiding and advising children rather than constantly telling them 'do this' or 'don't do that'; and letting them have a say in their own affairs once they are old enough. But he is also a firm father who insisted upon Charles sticking it out at Gordonstoun however much like a fish out of water he may have felt there. Indeed, the Queen Mother sometimes felt that he was too firm with her grandchildren, Charles in particular. But like a wise mother-in-law, she has refrained from interfering.

From his courtship days Philip's relationship with the Queen Mother has always been a warm one and at royal get-togethers they have often been seen closeted together in a corner, chuckling over some shared joke. He has a special regard, too, for Princess Alexandra, because she is the daughter of his cousin, Princess Marina, who did so much to promote his courtship. If he did not give her in marriage as he did Princess Margaret — Alexandra had a brother to do that for her — he did help to play host to the vast array of European Royals, many of them exiled, who flocked to Britain for her marriage to Angus Ogilvy. His contribution to the pre-wedding festivities was typically Philip.

[137]

He hired a couple of coaches, filled them with the visiting kings and queens, princes and princesses, and took them on a magical mystery tour of the English countryside. Just as he does not forget old friends, so he likes nothing better than to re-visit old ports of call and the stopping place for lunch that day was the *Hind's Head* at Bray, where he once used to stop off for a drink on his way back to Corsham from London. In those days he was a young naval officer earning a few pounds per week. Now he was Consort drawing (at that time) £40,000 a year. But his tastes had not changed all that much and, with his lunch, he ordered a pint of bitter 'in a pewter tankard, please'.

While conceding that publicity is an essential, if unlikeable, part of the royal round, Philip has always felt that a strict line should be drawn between public and private life. So he shared Elizabeth's view that there had been too much 'exposure' of Charles and Anne in childhood and that their third child, Andrew, should not suffer the same fate. Family life was going to be more private from now on. So there was no filming of the christening ceremony at which the child was named Andrew in memory of Philip's father. Nor were the photographs which Philip himself took with his new Hasselblad camera ever released. All the public got was an official photograph taken by Cecil Beaton. From now on, the royal parents were to do their utmost to keep the children out of the public eye. 'So that they can grow up as normally as possible,' Philip explained.

It was impossible, however, for him to keep himself out of the public eye. There was always something, it seemed, and much of it anti-Philip. If it wasn't something he had done, it was something he had said. Photographers sprinkled with water at the Chelsea Flower Show. Philip hadn't done it, said an official statement. But the public loved the thought that perhaps he had and general reaction was summed up by the wag who commented, 'I know he didn't do it, but he shouldn't do it again.' Other criticism was less lighthearted. His decision to accept the presidency of the World Wild Life Fund was labelled 'humbug' by the League Against Cruel Sports. A 1960 speech to the Anglo-German Association in which he advocated 'forgiving one's enemies' did not go down well with everyone. Australians were upset when he denounced kangaroo shooting. Greeks were offended when he said that he was born in Greece but was not Greek. A tiger shoot in India raised such a storm of criticism that it was perhaps fortunate that through injury he was unable to take part in a second hunt.

He was then, as now, a hard worker. It was as though he found it impossible to sit still. He was hardly ever at home, it seemed. In 1960, following Andrew's birth, he visited Canada and the United States. In 1961 it was back to India and Pakistan, this time as escort to his wife on one of her royal tours; and then to Nepal, Iran and Turkey. Later that year he was back in Ghana, accompanying Elizabeth on the visit she had been obliged to put off when she was pregnant with Andrew. He then went with her to Liberia, Sierra Leone and Gambia. In 1962 there was a solo eleven-country tour of South America during which he attended fifty receptions, twenty-two dinners and twelve luncheons, made thirty speeches, paid sixty-eight visits to plantations, mines, factories etc, laid eleven commemorative wreaths and one foundation stone. There were two more trips to Canada and the United States the same year and on one of them, in San Francisco, he ran into an old girl friend of his Venice days, now the matronly mother of four children. It was back to the United States the following year for the funeral of the assassinated John Kennedy, then off with his wife on yet another royal tour of Australia and New Zealand. He seemed indefatigable in his determination to show the flag, boost British exports and cement the ties of Commonwealth.

On the import side of royal affairs, there was a state visit to Britain by Philip's cousins, King Paul and Queen Frederika of Greece, which did not go down well in all quarters. Demonstrators were out in the streets and, on the evening of a palace banquet in the visitors' honour, even tried to scale the spike-topped railings of the royal home. One actually made it before ending up under arrest along with ninety-four others.

That state banquet was unusual in another respect – a little man with a stop-watch who clocked the time it took to carry the various courses from the vast basement kitchen to the banquet hall upstairs. He was one of a team of time-and-motion experts who spent several months seeing if it was possible to cut the cost of royal living. Philip has sometimes been accused of wasting money, but where Buckingham Palace is concerned, he has always felt that cash could be saved and it was hardly his fault if things did not work out quite as he envisaged. At the end of it all, royal footmen were told they must make their livery outfits last a year longer and gardeners were given the same instructions concerning their green baize aprons. But the number of servants actually went up slightly, not down. In due course, however, inflation was to secure what Philip's time-and-motion study had failed to achieve and in more recent years the palace staff has been cut by some fifteen per cent.

By this time, Philip was the most travelled prince in history, if not the most travelled man in the world. Certainly he was the most newsworthy, although son Charles has since tended to oust him from the headlines. But because whatever he may have achieved in travelling the world has been a matter of influence and atmosphere, both of which are unstatistical, he received little credit and few thanks. 'Prince Philip *Visits* Britain' was the welcome-home headline at the end of one overseas trip. It was the idiosyncrasies rather than the accomplishments which too often made the headlines. 'I raised my head and missed my shot,' a golfer grumbled to the newspapers after the Consort's helicopter broke his concentration while Philip was on his way to the Aldeburgh Festival.

Whatever Philip does or says has always been newsworthy and wherever he went at this time photographers and reporters were sure to follow. However, he had cause to be grateful for their presence the day his Flying Fifteen *Coweslip* capsized at Cowes. It was a photographers' launch which towed him in. To make a good story even better, Philip was standing on the jetty, watching *Coweslip* being winched out of the water, when the arm of the crane snapped. Philip looked up – and leapt aside in the nick of time as thirty feet of metal crashed down on the spot where he had been standing. 'That was a close shave', he said, calmly, to

Uffa Fox who was with him. Then there was his polo, a game he played with such abandon as to be extremely accident-prone. In 1960 it was a torn thigh muscle, in 1961 a broken ankle. In 1962 he suffered extensive bruising when he was thrown by his polo pony and in 1963 he gashed his left arm so badly it had to be stitched and he was forced to eat American-style for a time.

The broken ankle coincided with an ankle injury sustained by the Queen Mother. At a palace garden party that year, Philip could manage only to hobble. The Queen Mother, too, had to hobble. To the delight of those who witnessed the incident Elizabeth, too, emerged from the palace a moment later feigning a hobble in imitation of her husband and mother.

In The Red

Fatherhood, for Philip, has tended to be a somewhat protracted affair. He was in his twenties, in his first year of marriage, when his first son, Charles, was born. Now, in his sixtieth year, he has sixteen-year-old Edward, fourth child and third son, not yet off his hands. Philip was almost forty-three when Eddy, as he is called, was born in 1964 to complete the family circle. Whatever the circumstances of Andrew's birth, that of Edward would seem to have been the result of family planning, at least judging from something Elizabeth said not long after she had had Andrew. 'We'll have to think about having a little playmate for him.' With Charles, at the time, already away at boarding school and Anne soon to follow, she and Philip did not want Andrew raised as virtually an only child, she explained.

Delighted to find himself a father for the fourth time, Philip took photographs of his wife in bed with the new baby. In line with their new policy of personal privacy, the photographs were intended strictly for the family album. But somewhere along the line of developing and printing, someone ran off extra prints and these, to Philip's anger, found their way into magazines and newspapers around the world, though not until four years later.

Philip's cousin, King Paul, had just died in Greece and the day following Edward's birth, Philip, in company with Princess Marina, flew out there for the funeral. In consequence, the need to register the birth of the new baby quite slipped his mind. Legally, a birth in Britain has to be registered within forty-two days and there was only one more day to go to the legal deadline when the Caxton Hall registrar, appropriately named William Prince, was finally called to the palace.

If some people had thought Philip's earlier 'don't let's be beastly to the Germans' speech a shade premature, the British Government, by 1965, had come round to the same way of thinking. While Philip himself had taken advantage of his visits to British military establishments in Germany to call on his sisters, he had not yet – because the Queen's foreign trips must always be with the blessing of the Government – been able to take Elizabeth with him. But now at last, twenty years after the end of hostilities, the Government approved a visit.

Because the German trip was an official state visit, there was the inevitable pomp and ceremony; the unavoidable state functions. But in a weekend free from official junketing, Philip had the long-delayed pleasure of taking his wife to visit his sisters in their own homes. All three sisters were waiting to greet them as their train pulled into the wayside halt at Salem, the first passenger train to stop there in ten years. Theodore, now widowed, had her two grown-up sons, Max and Ludwig, with her. Margarita, also widowed, was accompanied by her eldest son, Kraft, while Sophie and her second husband, George, who lived with Theodora at Salem, had three children in tow. Philip's mother, turned eighty now, was there to complete the family reunion. Over the course of the weekend Philip took Elizabeth for a drive in an open carriage to show her something of the surrounding countryside and also to see the school he had attended in boyhood. The battered desk on which he had once hacked his initial was still there.

Margarita, of course, was eager that her royal sister-in-law should see her own home at Langenburg and on the Monday evening, after another day of official engagements, Philip took Elizabeth there. The evening somehow turned into a belated coming-of-age party for Margarita's twin sons, Ruprecht and Albrecht, who had celebrated their twenty-first birthday earlier that year.

There is a tendency to think of Philip as a rather unemotional man, a princely automaton going through the motions. He isn't like that. His emotions are as complex as those of any other man and perhaps more so than many. If anger and laughter are the two emotions he reveals most in public, there has been the odd occasion when something deeper and more intense has broken through, as when he visited Aberfan in the aftermath of the slag-heap disaster which killed 144 people, 116 of them children. He was ashen-faced as he picked his way through the wreckage, so moved emotionally that he would have jerked off his jacket and pitched in to help the rescue workers had it not been pointed out that to do so would inevitably have the effect of attracting sightseers which would hinder rather than help the job in hand.

He is a man who is devoted to his family, past and present; loyal to his friends. His friendship with Michael Parker survived the break of Parker's resignation. He hates the idea that people might think there was any justification for the verdict the revolutionary court in Greece passed on his dead father all those years ago. He has gone out of his way to help his sisters when they were financially distressed. And when his ageing mother was taken ill not long after that family reunion in Germany, he flew out there personally to bring her back to Britain and arranged for her admission to hospital. Later, when she came out of hospital, she was given her own suite of rooms at Buckingham Palace. Philip was in and out to see her all the time and at Christmas that year, with his mother still not well enough to go to Windsor with the rest of the family, he drove Elizabeth back to London on Christmas Day to take his mother her gifts and have tea with her.

If Philip's speech on patching things up with Germany had been thought controversial and premature, one he made about Rhodesia about this time was to prove a lot more so. In retrospect, what he said on the subject would seem to have been mild and sensible enough. 'In the long run it is better to spin out the process of the solution of these difficulties with patience and, therefore, with a bit of luck to get a peaceful solution, rather than risk a bloodbath and many other unpredictable results by forcing the pace at this moment.' But there was the usual rush of blood to the head in some quarters. Lord Brockway, chairman of the Movement for Colonial Freedom, prophesied that Philip's speech would have 'a very unfortunate effect upon Africa and the unity of the Commonwealth.' In the event, circumstances were to compel the spinning-out process which Philip advocated – it took another fifteen years for Rhodesia to become Zimbabwe – and the Commonwealth would appear to have survived.

Not that everything has gone Philip's way all the time. Invited to apply for election to the Institute of Physics and the Physical Society, he had the embarrassment, when he did so, of having his application turned down. However, there was compensation in being awarded the medal of the Institute of Public Relations for 'his magnificent service to public relations and mutual understanding, particularly during his visit to the United States.' That particular visit was in 1966 and took him to Miami, Houston, Dallas, Palm Springs, Los Angeles and New York.

Always an involved father, he journeyed to Gordonstoun with Elizabeth to see Charles take part in a school production of *Macbeth*. For once, the son outshone the father. Philip, in his day, was given only the minor role of Donalbain. Charles, magnificently, if falsely, bearded, had the title role. Father was similarly at the Badminton Horse Trials to see daughter Anne complete a clear round and win £5 for her trouble, a juvenile forerunner to the European Evening Championship which was to come her way later.

Anne was still at Benenden at the time. When she left school there were to be a few problems. She had no clear idea of what she wanted to do with her life, had hardly any friends, and few opportunities to meet boys of her own age. Far from enjoying her teenage years, she became extremely depressed. It was Philip who pinpointed what was wrong and did something about it. He had a quiet word or two with polo-playing friends who had offspring of around Anne's age. The result was a sudden welter of invitations and, for a time, an almost non-stop round of parties, discos and theatre-going which helped Anne through a difficult phase of her young life and, as an unavoidable by-product, supplied the newspapers with some good copy along the way.

Charles was now on the verge of young manhood and the

earlier father-son relationship between him and Philip began to merge into something more like the relationship between older and younger brothers. 'A great help,' Charles recalls his father being at this time. 'A strong influence.' It could hardly be otherwise with a father of Philip's forceful personality. He passed on to his son some sound advice to ensure princely success: Stand up straight, speak out and look people straight in the eye. Especially straight in the eye, it seems, if they are an attractive female in a low-cut dress. Otherwise, as Charles was to tell movie actress Susan Hampshire on some future occasion, there is always the danger of a photographer sneaking up and catching you in what might appear to be 'a compromising attitude'.

Certainly Charles was old enough by now to have some say in his own future. Philip once boasted that he was 'one of those stupid bums who never went to university.' All the same, he went out of his way to help when Charles opted for university. 'He was keen to go, so we tried to figure out a way.' Figuring out a way, when your son is also heir to his mother's throne, is no simple matter. A lot of other people had to be brought into the act, among them prime minister Harold Wilson, the Archbishop of Canterbury, and Dr Robin Woods, Dean of Windsor. Philip chaired a small top-level conference at the palace. Uncle Dickie was also present, on this occasion not because he was a member of the family but to ensure that the armed forces were not overlooked in planning the heir to the throne's future.

The decision of the conference was largely to leave things to the boy's parents, subject to the advice of Dr Woods. As a result, Charles went in due course to Trinity College, Cambridge, where his grandfather – if not his father – had been before him. Philip was happy enough about that, but less happy with the idea of staging a sort of mini-coronation ceremony at Caernarvon at which Charles would be formally invested as Prince of Wales. 'Is this sort of virtually mediaeval revival really necessary?' he queried. 'Isn't it all a little archaic?' Not only archaic, but of questionable origin. Until the wily Welsh wizard, David Lloyd George, who saw it as a political vote-catcher, sold the idea to George V in the days when the late Duke of Windsor was Prince of Wales, it is doubtful whether there had ever been such a ceremony at Caernarvon. A few hot-headed Welsh nationalists shared Philip's doubts and said so with bombs in the run-up to the ceremony. But everything was all right on the day, with Philip giving his eldest son a reassuring grin as pomp and circumstance ran its course.

That was in 1969, a year which saw the death of Philip's sister, Theodora, and in the December of his mother. His cousin, Princess Marina, to whom he was always so close, had died the previous year. It was also the year which saw the screening of the television film *Royal Family*.

Unlike the idea for the Queen's Gallery, a changing public display of paintings from the Royal Collection which Philip had conceived back in 1962, the credit for *Royal Family* was not his alone. It arose out of conversations with Uncle Dickie, whose television series – *The Life & Times of Earl Mountbatten* – had already been successfully screened. Philip seized on the idea as a way of burnishing the royal image, which was somewhat in the doldrums at the time. There was the added attraction of almost certain profits which would help to bolster royal finances, already beginning to feel the pinch of inflation. The television authorities, once they were allowed in on the act, were all for it, of course. The Royals at work and play, at home, relaxing, just being themselves, perhaps even eating fish and chips like any other family. That would bump up the ratings – not that ratings counted for much in what was to be a joint BBC-ATV venture. Still, they could hardly wait. Elizabeth, initially, was rather less enthused, but Philip managed to convince her and, later, when she saw herself on the screen, she was highly delighted.

Philip, of course, kept the whole business under close personal control – or tried to – heading a production committee which included Mountbatten's film producer son-in-law, Lord Brabourne; William Heseltine, an Australian with something of Mike Parker's breezy outlook who had now taken over from Richard Colville as the palace press officer; and representatives of the BBC (Richard Cawston) and ATV (Robin Gill). All the same, there were times during the eleven months it took to shoot the film when he perhaps had cause to regret that he had started it all. After all his earlier objections to the activities of 'peeping Tom' photographers, he now had to sit back and take it while television cameras peeped away for all they were worth. And they were there at his own request. 'Too bloody close,' he protested vigorously when he felt they were getting more than their money's worth.

But the ends, financial and otherwise, were to justify the means. In Britain some twenty-three million viewers gaped awe-struck at their screens when the film was first televised. There were a further fifteen million viewers the second time around, though some of them may have been fervent loyalists sitting it through twice. In the United States alone the sale price handsomely covered the cost of production and distribution, with the palace's share of the eventual profits proving a welcome windfall as royal finances felt the pinch of inflation more and more.

In an era when other people's pay-packets were starting to go up by leaps and bounds to cope with Britain's inflationary cost of living, the Royals were still struggling to make ends meet on the Civil List annuities allocated by Parliament when the Queen first ascended the throne in 1952 – £475,000 a year to her to cover the cost of Monarchy and £40,000 to Philip to run his own sideshow as Consort. With royal servants wanting larger pay-packets, royal aides feeling they were getting left behind in the matter of salaries, garden parties, banquets all costing more, half-share of the film's profits, said to be around £100,000, did not go far. Something else had to be done if the Royal Family were not to file a petition in bankruptcy . . . and an interview on American television set the ball rolling.

Philip had gone on to the United States from Canada, where he also delivered what he saw as a few home-truths. 'It is a complete misconception to imagine that the Monarchy exists in the interest of the Monarchy. It does not. It exists in the interest of the people in the sense that we do not come here for the benefit of our health, so to speak. We can think of other ways of enjoying ourselves. Judging by some of the programme we are required to do here, and considering how little we get out of it, you can assume that it is done in the interests of the Canadian people and not our own interest.'

And so to Washington, where a television interview was recorded for the NBC's *Meet The Press* programme. The question of royal finances came up. 'We go into the red next year,' Philip replied, bluntly, 'which is not bad housekeeping if you come to think of it. We have, in fact, kept the thing going on a budget which was based on the costs of eighteen years ago. So there have been very considerable corners that have had to be cut and it's beginning to have its effect. There's no question of we just get a lump sum and we can do what we like with it. The thing is that it's allocated for particular purposes. Now, inevitably, if nothing happens we shall either. . . . I don't know . . . we may have to move into smaller premises, who knows? We've closed down . . . well, for instance, we had a small yacht which we've had to sell (his ocean-racing yawl *Bloodhound* bought for £11,000 seven years earlier) and I shall have to give up polo fairly soon (he did, but not for reasons of finance), things like that. I'm on a different allowance anyway, but I've also been on it for the last eighteen years.'

Even before it was shown on British television, the interview caused an uproar back home. As always, some politicians were less incensed by what had been said than by who had said it; others by the fact that it had been said abroad in the first place. It was left to an American to spring to Philip's defence. In an open letter to the British people, published in a national newspaper, a supportive New Yorker eulogised Philip as 'this man of extraordinary intellect and articulation' doing more 'to uphold everything we like and admire about Britain than a whole army of politicians and pressmen.'

If no commercial firm had the enterprise or nerve to offer to sponsor Philip's polo-playing, as British Leyland was later to sponsor his son-in-law's eventing, London dockers had a whip-round on his behalf. He could, of course, hardly accept their money and suggested that they should give it to a dockside boys' club instead. And in Parliament, the Prime Minister stumbled his way through a somewhat ambiguous statement which endeavoured to explain that the Government was already helping the Royals out while at the same time saying that a Select Committee would be set up to look into the whole question of palace finances.

It was in the aftermath of all this that Philip went along to a luncheon given by the Small Businessmen's Association. Having Philip as its guest-of-honour, the Association decided to get all the mileage it could out of the occasion by inviting the press along also. An official of the Association said later that the presence of reporters had been cleared in advance with Buckingham Palace. Apparently no one bothered to tell Philip. So what he had to say over lunch, as far as he was concerned, was private and off-the-cuff. What he did say is a matter of dispute. It was to do with the Welsh singer Tom Jones, one of the stars of the previous night's Royal Variety Show which Philip had sat through. Philip was to say later that his lunchtime criticism was directed at the choice of songs – not the singer. Others thought he was sniping at the singer rather than the songs. Either way, the phrase 'bloody awful' was used.

All of which might not have mattered if Philip, having said whatever he said, had not spotted a reporter taking note of his remarks. 'What the hell are you doing?' he demanded. With which he came to his feet and stalked out of the room. In the lobby another reporter was already telephoning the story. Philip heaved open the door of the phone box and demanded to know 'what the bloody hell' he was doing while embarrassed Association officials scuttled around him, promising to 'stop' the report. 'You'd bloody well better,' Philip told them.

However, all's well that ends well. Philip later apologised to the press and there was a note of 'explanation', as distinct from apology, to Tom Jones. The matter of royal finances was to end well, too, though the Select Committee took a good deal longer to complete its work. It was not until 1971 that the Civil List was more than doubled to £980,000, more or less in line with the 106 per cent increase in the cost of living since the Queen came to the throne in 1952. Philip's own money went up at the same time, though not quite to the same extent. He got £65,000 that year. Increases since, though by no means in line with inflation, have enabled the Monarchy more less to sustain the style to which it has become accustomed. Whether it would have done so without Philip's remarks on American television is anybody's guess.

Signs Of The Times

Most amateurs who indulge over-enthusiastically in their particular sport pay the penalty sooner or later; arthritis, fibrositis, cartilage trouble, etc. With Philip it was synovitis, a form of arthritis resulting in inflamed membranes, of the right wrist. Treatment, including the use of Butazolidin, more commonly known as 'bute' in horsey circles, enabled him to keep on with his polo playing during the 1970 season, during which he took another nasty tumble resulting in torn shoulder ligaments. He had to call off a few engagements and go around for a time with his arm in a sling. But he could only ease the stiffness and soreness of his overworked wrist, not cure the underlying condition and, in 1971, about the time of his fiftieth birthday, he was reluctantly compelled to call it a day where polo was concerned. He could console himself with the knowledge that he had enjoyed a pretty good playing career since those early days under Uncle Dickie's tutelage in Malta; achieving a handicap of four, captaining the Windsor Park team and playing for England.

Being Philip, of course, he had to take up something else in place of polo. He toyed with the idea of golf, but hitting a stationary ball while standing still seemed rather tame after taking swipes at a ball from the back of a galloping polo pony. It was thanks to Lieutenant Colonel (later Sir) John Miller, the Crown Equerry (which means that he is responsible for overseeing the cars and coaches in the royal mews and the chauffeurs and coachmen who drive them), that he developed an interest in carriage driving.

The Crown Equerry was himself already of international

standard even if there were, at that time, no top-flight international events. However, there is nothing like royal interest in something to make it really take off and Philip's new enthusiasm for the sport was instrumental, in part at least, for the first-ever world championship. It was held in Germany in 1972. Colonel Miller drove the royal team. Philip was not yet good enough for that. Still, he was improving quickly and, under Miller's tuition, he drove a phaeton drawn by two Cleveland Bays in the Windsor Horse Show that year and carried off the first prizes in two events arranged by the British Driving Society.

Having successfully mastered the knack of handling two-in-hand, he promptly graduated to four-in-hand, driving with much the same aggressive dash and daring that he had earlier demonstrated on the polo field and in games of deck hockey aboard the royal yacht. And sometimes with the same almost inevitable results. He was shaken and bruised when his wagonette overturned in the grounds of Windsor Castle, with one of the horses managing to get a kick in as he fell. Within weeks he was hurt again, though not seriously, while taking part in a three-day event at Lowther Castle. One of the horses collided with a tree stump, the carriage overturned and Philip and the rest of the occupants were pitched out. All of which did nothing to diminish his enthusiasm for this new sport. 'He is always ringing me up and asking for four-in-hand driving to be included in the Olympics,' Lord Killanan, president of the International Olympic Federation, grumbled good-naturedly.

If Philip, at fifty, was still as lean and active as ever, and arguably as handsome, there were signs on all sides of the march of middle age. His two elder offspring were children no longer. Eighteen years after gaining his own 'wings', he journeyed to RAF College Cranwell to see son Charles presented with his. Delighted to learn that Charles had revealed a natural aptitude for flying, had excelled at jet-batics and had the makings of a first-class fighter pilot, Philip was as affable that day as anyone remembers seeing him. He even managed an exchange of quips with the ever-present photographers. Would he mind being photographed shaking hands with his son? 'I'll stand on my head if you want me to', Philip grinned, though it was perhaps as well that no one took him at his word.

He was in equally high spirits at Burghley when his daughter, thought to be too out of practice or out of condition for inclusion in the British team due to a recent spell in hospital, entered the European Three-Day Event off her own bat and ended up beating not only the team from which she had been excluded but the cream of riders from Ireland, France, Italy and Russia. 'I'm only here for the beer,' joked Philip. But a father's pride showed through.

In 1972 he and Elizabeth celebrated their silver wedding anniversary. Where had those twenty-five years all gone? Inevitably, the celebrations became public property. There was a state drive through London, a thanksgiving service at Westminister Abbey (where they were married), a walk-about (the first in Britain) at the Barbican, with a celebration lunch thrown by the Lord Mayor of London at the Guildhall. Gifts streamed in as they had done on the occasion of the wedding, silver wine coasters from the Cabinet, silver toast racks from the Diplomatic Corps, an antique silver basket (for the royal yacht) from the Board of Admiralty, silver spurs from the Lords Lieutenant and so on. Elizabeth got only one spur (to wear when riding side-saddle at her annual Birthday Parade), but Philip got a pair. He grinned as broadly as anyone when his wife opened her thank-you speech at the Guildhall with the words, 'I think that every-body really will concede that on this, of all days, I should begin my speech with the words "My husband and I".' Those satiric words may even have been his idea. On a more personal level, Charles and Anne arranged a celebration party for their parents at the palace at which 200 friends and relatives were present.

Among the guests at that silver wedding party was a young man named Mark Phillips. The following New Year he was invited to Sandringham and Philip took him out shooting, just as Elizabeth's father had once taken him. Later, after Mark had left to rejoin his regiment, Anne brought up the question of marriage. Philip liked Mark well enough, he said, and was 'very happy' with the idea. The courtship which followed was very different from Philip's own. But, then, times had changed. For Philip there had been only rare opportunities to be alone with Elizabeth. Nearly always there had been someone around, her parents, sister Margaret, servants. Anne and Mark were constantly off on their own together. Philip and his future in-laws had seen each other often, if at intervals, and come to know each other well during the nearly four years which elapsed between his first wartime visit to Windsor and his ultimate betrothal to the King's daughter. He could hardly have come to know Mark as well during a couple of weekends at Sandringham and another at Windsor which was about all they saw of each other.

Still, Mark acted correctly. There is no record of when and where, or even whether, Philip asked King George VI formally for his daughter's hand. It seems to have been Elizabeth who mainly badgered her father in to letting them get married. But Mark did things on the formally correct level, even if he was in some doubt initially as to whether it was his future mother-in-law's consent he needed rather than Philip's. After all, she was the Queen. But Elizabeth, mindful of her husband's masculine pride, has always deferred to him on a personal level and in family matters. So it was to Philip, as Anne's father, that Mark addressed his request. Just as Philip was once in awe of Elizabeth's father, so was Mark in awe of Philip. He recalls feeling extremely nervous – 'petrified' is his own word – as he was ushered into the Consort's small sitting room overlooking the rose garden at Windsor. He need not have worried. Philip can be affability itself on the right occasion and, at the right time, kind and understanding. And this was just such an occasion.

Elizabeth wanted a private celebration, a family get-together, before the betrothal was made public. Less easy than it sounds. Mark would have to get leave from his regiment. Charles would have to fly home from the West Indies where he was serving aboard HMS *Minerva*. Andrew and Eddy would have to be on vacation from school. The Queen Mother must be there too, of course. Tricky to arrange if the cat was not to be let out of the bag in the process, but Philip, liking nothing so much as hoodwinking the newspapers, enjoyed every minute of the several subterfuges involved. The get-together could hardly take place at the palace without Fleet Street getting wind of it. Windsor was no better. Scotland was the place – if they could all get there without it becoming obvious that it was a gathering of the clan. To avoid taking too many servants north from Buckingham Palace (which might have given the game away), he arranged for the family to stay not at Balmoral Castle, as usual, but at Craig Gowan House, a smaller and more easily manageable residence nearby. So it was planned. Anne, returning from a visit to Spain, was joined at the airport by her mother and together they flew on to Scotland. Mark drove north on the pretext that he was simply visiting a fellow-officer who happened to live in Scotland. Charles flew back from the Indies, Andrew was fetched from Gordonstoun and the Queen Mother went on holiday to Birkhall, within easy driving distance. So the royal clan gathered and when the gathering was complete Philip loaded his barbecue gear into a Land Rover and off they all went for a picnic amidst the heather.

On the public side of royal affairs, Philip continued to work as hard as ever. Too hard, his aides were inclined to think sometimes. There were times when he returned from a non-stop day of travel and speech-making looking desperately tired, more ready than he had been simply to flop into the nearest available chair. His curiosity was still as insatiable as ever, his desire to try anything new still strong. Returning from a ninety-minute flight in Concorde over the Bay of Biscay, he was eager to get at the controls. The supersonic silver dart was at 51,000 feet, flying at 1304 mph, twice the speed of sound, when Philip took over. He was at the controls for up to thirty minutes before reducing speed to subsonic level and handing back to test pilot Brian Trubshaw for the landing at Fairford. Philip was always one of Concorde's most enthusiastic supporters. 'Don't talk to me about smoke and noise,' he retorted, half-jokingly, to those who moaned about the aircraft. 'I have Windsor Castle at one end of Heathrow and Buckingham Palace not far from the other.'

If he made few concessions to middle age where work was concerned, there was, perhaps, an inclination to take things a little more easily in the leisure field. Though not where carriage driving was concerned. He went at that as enthusiastically as he had once charged about the polo field. But at Sandringham there was less bird-shooting and more bird-watching. He set up a nature sanctuary there and would often go out on his own to wander the fields and marshes with camera and binoculars in place of a gun. He was out on the marshes on one occasion when he was spotted by a look-out posted to keep any chance wayfarer from blundering into an area where birds were being netted and ringed for a wildfowl survey. 'Steer clear, mate,' the look-out called, waving him away, and Philip obligingly changed course. It was only as he came nearer that the embarrassed look-out realised he had been shouting at the Consort.

Oil painting was an increasingly favourite form of relaxation. He had continued to dabble in it ever since his Antarctic excursion aboard *Britannia* in the company of Edward Seago. It had become his habit if a scene took his fancy in the course of his world-wide travels – in Australia, Malaysia, India, Pakistan, wherever – to block it out or make a rough sketch to be turned later into a finished painting, often during the long summer vacation at Balmoral. If he was not satisfied with the end-product it was left to gather dust against the studio walls. But some of his efforts merited better treatment. His wife liked one of his paintings sufficiently to have it framed and hung in her sitting room at Windsor. Charles managed to acquire some of his father's paintings of Sandringham and Anne has some of Windsor Castle. Close friends were also favoured with the occasional gift painting, though only the friends know who the artist is. More modest than you might think where his art-work is concerned, Philip has no desire for his signature to give his paintings an unrealistic value and declines to sign them. He was modest, too, when invited to exhibit some of his work at the 1976 Royal Academy exhibition. He agreed to show four of his paintings – Windsor Castle, the Queen Mother's Castle of Mey, fishermen's huts in Malaysia and a steel mill in India – but insisted that they were hung in the entrance hall rather than included in the exhibition proper. One art expert who viewed them came up with the following critique: 'He has a simple style, not sophisticated. They are very much an amateur's work. He does not seem to use a wide range of brushes, but there is a lot of promise there.'

He took time out from an official trip to Scotland that same year to pay a nostalgic return visit to Rosyth, where he was once based as a young naval officer. Now it was his eldest son who was based there as the newly-appointed skipper of an ancient timber-built minehunter, HMS *Bronington*. Promoted to the rank of lieutenant after a little over four years in the Navy, Charles rated his own ship at the age of twenty-seven, which was two years younger than Dad had been when he took command of *Magpie* more than a quarter of a century earlier. He had just returned from a night exercise and the stubble of the new beard he was growing at the time sandpapered his chin as he welcomed his Admiral of the Fleet father aboard and showed him round. Not that there was all that much to show. His little minehunter was only 153 feet from stem to stern, which is a good deal less than half the length of *Britannia*.

Middle-aged or not, Philip continued to rush around the world as frenetically as ever. Island-hopping trips had long since become a regular part of his work-load and in 1971 there was another – to the Galapagos Islands, Easter Island, Pitcairn Island, Cook Island and half-a-dozen other such places as well as Australia. He was also in France, Hungary, Iran and Sweden that year as well as accompanying Elizabeth on yet another trip to Canada and a state visit to Turkey. In 1972 he was again beside her on a tour of Thailand, Singapore, Malaysia and a number of other places as well as on a state visit to Yugoslavia. All of which did not prevent him taking off on his own to Kenya, Belgium, to West Germany for the Olympic Games and to Denmark for the funeral of King Frederik. In 1973 he was in Thailand again (solo this time), Singapore, India, Afghanistan and the Soviet Union, a new name in the royal travelogue. As though all that was not enough, there were two more trips to Canada with his wife and yet another to Australia. After all, Elizabeth is Queen of Canada and Australia along with New Zealand and some dozen other places scattered around the globe as well as the United Kingdom. And Philip is her indefatigable Consort. They were together on a state visit to Indonesia in 1974 when there was a telephone call for Philip in Jakarta. It was Princess Anne on the line from Buckingham Palace to tell him of the attempt to kidnap her as she and husband Mark were on their way back from a charity film show. Four people – Anne's bodyguard, chauffeur, a policeman and a passing journalist – were gunned down, though all lived to tell the tale, before a burly Cockney intervened to knock down the would-be kidnapper. 'It was incredible,' Anne said. 'The sort of thing one can't believe is really happening.'

Philip was anxious for details, of course, but Anne was still shaken from the experience and there was not a great deal she could tell him. She remembered the would-be kidnapper saying, 'I'll get a couple of million' and 'I only want you for two days.'

Having assured himself that his daughter and son-in-law were unharmed, Philip woke Elizabeth – it was five o'clock in the morning in Jakarta – to tell her what had happened. In the strict show-must-go-on tradition of Monarchy, Queen and Consort decided to complete their state visit to Indonesia before flying back to London three days later.

There was a time in the 1970s when it seemed as if Philip had decided to forego controversy and settle for a quiet life in the future. Or perhaps it was that the newspapers were far too pre-occupied with the love life of son Charles to find space for father's speeches. But Philip was still there, brooding a little perhaps, seeing clearer than some what was wrong with Britain, but lacking the power to do anything about it . . . except make speeches.

Consistently, over the years, he has exhorted his adopted nation to greater effort, telling industrialists as far back as 1961 that 'it is about time we pulled our finger out' and saying, with a degree of exasperation in 1967, that he was 'sick and tired of making excuses for this country'. The 1970s found him increasingly concerned with Britain's downhill drift. Just as he once said that he would go anywhere to raise money for the National Playing Fields Association and on another occasion that he would make any sacrifice for the benefit of the Commonwealth, so it now seemed as if he was prepared to say anything which might help to jolt Britain out of its apathy. He denounced 'controls, restrictions and limitations', pointed out that Britain was rapidly approaching the position of 'a man living beyond his means' and sneered that 'anyone who thinks that North Sea oil alone is going to get us out of trouble would also believe that social security is available at a pawnbroker's shop'. All good, clean, fighting stuff, though not always well received in some quarters. Undeterred, Philip continued making speeches, giving interviews writing articles, all on much the same theme. He even took part in the Jimmy Young radio show on Radio 2. British industry he said on the programme, was like a team 'with eleven coaches sitting on the bench and one player trying to compete with the opposition'. The station's switchboard was promptly swamped with calls. 'An amazing response,' said Jimmy Young, 'with most people seeming to say that what Britain needs is a managing director and that Philip is the man for the job.'

Sometimes, as in an interview with America's prestigious *News & World Report*, he was optimistic about Britain's future, insisting that the country would yet bounce back. 'The adaptability and flexibility is still there.' Other times, as in an hour-long broadcast on Radio Clyde which he taped himself while on holiday at Balmoral, he was a prophet of doom and gloom, warning that by the year 2,000 Britain could be a totalitarian state in which 'black markets will flourish while the major financial and commercial markets will decline . . . the take-home element of wages and salaries will become relatively less important as all the major necessities will be provided out of taxation . . . dependence on fringe benefits associated with employment and trades unions will increase. It is worth bearing in mind that slavery is no more than a system of directed labour and fringe benefits.' Like so many of Philip's utterances it brought echoes of 'Splendid stuff' from the Conservative side of the House of Commons and an ominous 'All that is doomed is the system of purchased privilege he has enjoyed all his life' from Labour's Neil Kinnock.

As always, he was frequently in hot water. Undeterred, he went on sailing perilously close to the political barrier royalty is traditionally supposed to avoid. He was denounced as 'socially irresponsible' by Nicholas Fogg, editor of *Christian Action*, for a speech in Edinburgh in which he said, 'We subsidise people to have children. You could argue that it would be more practical to tax people for having children.'

Surprisingly, he found himself with some unexpected allies as the result of a speech he made to the Royal Commonwealth Agricultural Society. He spoke about 'crude industrial philosophies in agriculture' having immense social and demographic consequences. Then he added 'I think it is a thing which this country is about to discover what it feels like if and when it joins the Common Market.'

Was he warning Britain against going into the Common Market? Some people thought so and Philip found a strange assortment of bedfellows suddenly springing to his support, among them Member of Parliament Willie Hamilton, not exactly noted for his fondness for the Royals in other respects. 'Probably for the first time in my life I agree with the sentiments Prince Philip has expressed,' said Hamilton. Another Labourite, Eric Heffer, thought Philip unwise to have said what he did, but nevertheless felt that 'there is a great deal of commonsense in it'.

Perhaps it was the odd company in which he so unexpectedly found himself which caused Philip to act so quickly in assuring the Government of the day that what he had said was in no way intended politically. A statement issued by his office insisted that he was 'disturbed to think that his remarks have been interpreted as being anti-Common Market in tone. The Duke of Edinburgh has always been very careful not to express any opinion on this subject. The context of his remarks on this occasion was the danger of treating agriculture as if it were simply a manufacturing industry'.

Misinterpreted, then? Apparently so. But is it always simply a case of misinterpretation? That Philip sometimes finds his position frustrating was revealed when he turned down an invitation to take part in a debate on Monarchy at Oxford university. He couldn't, he said, because he was barred from 'practising free speech on matters loosely termed political'. He was even more blunt, on another occasion, to students at Edinburgh university. 'I know all about freedom of speech because I get kicked in the teeth often enough for saying things I am told I damned well ought not to say.' That was said on the spur of the moment. With a man of Philip's forceful character, it is perhaps not impossible that other things, too, are said on the spur of the moment on subjects about which he feels strongly.

If Philip's speech to the Royal Commonwealth Agricultural Society was to be the first time Willie Hamilton had agreed with him, it was, perhaps, also the last. Certainly things seemed back to normal between them when Philip wrote an article for the magazine *Engineer* which concluded: 'The welfare state is a protection against failure and exploitation, but national recovery can take place only if innovators and men of enterprise and hard work can prosper.' Retorted Hamilton: 'Nobody has done better out of the welfare state than the Prince, his family and relatives.'

The biggest furore of all was to come early in 1977 – the year of Elizabeth's silver jubilee. What became known as Philip's 'dry rot' interview in the magazine *Director* raised parliamentary left-wingers to a fresh pitch of frenzy. In it Philip compared Britain's economic position with dry rot in a house. . . . 'You don't know when it starts, you don't know when the crisis is, but gradually the place becomes uninhabitable.' All in all, it was a reasoned – and reasonable – interview, if peppered with Philip-isms: 'We have tried to assume that human nature is different from what it is. Because you don't like the idea of people being avaricious, you can't simply say that avariciousness doesn't exist any more.' . . . 'Some people obviously do think you can have a totally egalitarian system. But no one has achieved one yet above the level of a tribal society.' . . . 'If you clobber savings income . . . you take people out of investing in industrials and you force them into things like jewellery, pictures, china and *objets d'art.* Even the trade unions are doing it.'

Such was the fury exhibited in the House of Commons over these comments – Philip was called everything from 'a British joke' to 'one of the best-kept security claimants in the country' to 'impudent and ill-advised' – that the Speaker, George Thomas, was obliged to bring proceedings to a temporary halt. The Consort, he said, must be spoken of 'in courteous language'.

High Finance

On 6 February 1977, it was exactly twenty-five years since Elizabeth had ascended the throne on the death of her father (though silver jubilee celebrations were deferred until summer when it might possibly be fine for a few days) and Philip had become her Consort as well as her husband. Left-wing Members of Parliament picked that day to have another go at Philip in the House of Commons. Or, rather, it was picked for them.

The cause of the row this time was not something Philip had said or even done, but the fact that he was getting more money, an increase of £20,000 to £85,000 for the year. His wife's Civil List payment had gone up, too, and by a great deal more. Payments to the Queen Mother, Princess Anne and Princess Margaret had similarly been increased to cushion them against inflation. But as so often, it was Philip – the perennial 'baddy' in the royal soap opera – who got most of the stick. Tom Litterick's attack on him was particularly vitriolic, labelling the Consort 'a useless, reactionary, arrogant parasite'.

Harking back to the Parliamentary furore of the previous month, which followed the interview with Philip published in *Director*, Litterick said, 'Two weeks ago, Philip, the most well-paid social security claimant in Britain, told us we paid too much attention to the poor and not enough to the deserving rich. I would like to hear his comments on his own £20,000 a year wage increase for being his wife's husband.'

'His wife's husband' is one way of phrasing it. 'For being Consort' is another. As Consort, at the last count available at this writing,* his money was up to £135,000 for the year. But let's get it straight – it isn't all pocket money. 'I'm self-employed,' Philip says. And so, in a sense, he is. Like any other self-employed person, what is his is only what is left over after paying the expenses of the business. He pays the salaries of his aides: Private Secretary, Assistant Private Secretary, Chief Clerk and Accountant. Because he needs them constantly on tap, he also pays the rent and rates of accommodation near the palace for them and their telephone bills. He pays the wages of his two valets, but his security men come free (at least as far as he is concerned). Because he makes use of royal cars for public functions, he also thinks it right and proper to meet the upkeep of two of them, pay the chauffeurs and buy their uniforms. As with his security men, the use of aircraft and helicopters of the Queen's Flight comes free. He buys his own uniforms, naval, aerial, military, pays for his own laundry, pays for the goodwill gifts – wallets, cufflinks etc – he distributes and has to find not only his own tips wherever he goes but also, again because he thinks it right and proper, those of his entourage. Like many other self-employed people, he gets a few perks, of course, principally the fact that he doesn't have to pay for his food and keep.

There, at least from the financial viewpoint, the similarity between Philip and any other self-employed person ends. Other self-employed are obliged to make an annual, and fairly detailed profit-and-loss return to the Inland Revenue, backed up with bank statements, receipted bills, petty cash slips and an accountant's certificate if necessary. Philip doesn't. Instead, the Inland Revenue agree on a balance between the expenses of the job and personal income. Details of this agreement are naturally as confidential as anyone else's tax affairs, but is believed to be something of the order of 60–40. Whatever it is, Philip pays tax on that part regarded as his personal income.

He also has one other big advantage over other British husbands. Unlike them, he is not legally responsible for any tax accruing from his wife's invested income. As Queen, Elizabeth

* Civil List, March 1980.

[165]

pays no tax. Not that he worries much about money. With a state hand-out of £135,000 this year, and probably more next, he hardly needs to, you may think. But then, he didn't worry about it when he was a young naval officer on a few pounds a week either.

Attacking Philip on the anniversary of the Queen's accession proved to be poor tactics on Litterick's part. Over the course of the next few days he found himself inundated with letters and telephone calls. The letters were mostly critical, some abusive, while the calls were 'disgusting, obscene and threatening'.

In his early years as Consort, when he looked almost like a young Greek (or Scandinavian) god, Philip's popularity was undoubted and widespread. In recent years it has been more difficult to assess. Charles would appear to have taken over from Dad in the royal male popularity stakes with Andrew coming up fast. But that is just an impression. There are no official statistics, of course. Lacking official statistics, the fact that Tom Litterick analysed the first batch of letters which streamed in following his House of Commons outburst is valuable. Of that first batch, fifty-nine agreed with Litterick and 160 disagreed, some abusively so. On a percentage basis, that gave Philip a seventy-three per cent popularity rating, which is quite something after twenty-five controversial years as Consort.

Every year is a busy one for Philip. But that year of 1977 was even busier than usual. Caught up in the silver jubilee celebrations of his wife's twenty-five years on the throne, he accompanied her on visits to the countries of the Commonwealth – Australia, New Zealand, Samoa, Tonga, Fiji. He later journeyed with her on celebratory royal progresses throughout much of England, Wales and Scotland as well as on a quick visit to troubled Northern Ireland. Inevitably, it was Elizabeth who was nearly always the limelight. It was her silver jubilee, not his, though he had been Consort for as long as she had been Queen, and he deliberately maintained a low profile. However, his gift for quickfire repartee was noticeable on walkabouts and during their progress through Scotland it seems that he could not resist attempting to rival Willie McGonagall, the nineteenth-century

Scottish poetaster who once trudged fifty miles to Balmoral to present a batch of his verses to Queen Victoria, only to find himself turned away at the gates.

The occasion was in Dundee, where McGonagall once worked as a weaver. Regulars of the Windmill Bar there, after seeing Elizabeth and Philip go by, were moved to imitate McGonagall, penning a few verses to mark the occasion and handing them to a royal aide for onward transmission. To their delighted surprise, a few days later, they received a reply, also in verse, on the official notepaper of the Palace of Holyroodhouse, royal headquarters in Edinburgh, and signed 'Philip'. Said the Scottish Office subsequently, 'We have checked with Prince Philip and he did write the poem. It is definitely genuine.'

'Poem' is perhaps rating it a little highly. Judge for yourselves (though space permits us to reproduce only part of it):

> *'I recall very well the pub on the hill,*
> *Which now I see was the old Windmill;*
> *It wasn't the crowd coming out of the door*
> *That caught my eye at quarter past four,*
> *'Twas the Ann Street windows attracted my stare,*
> *I wondered if anyone could be living up there;*
> *Then seeing the smiles on your customers' faces,*
> *I reckon your pub was one of those places*
> *Where the noise of good cheer drives off all dull cares*
> *And makes it impossible to live up those stairs.'*

Switching uniforms, donning morning suit or evening dress as the occasion might require, Philip helped Elizabeth host Commonwealth heads of state at a palace banquet, was with her for the Trooping the Colour ceremony in London and the Knights of the Garter parade at Windsor, the Royal Air Force review at Finningley and the Royal Navy review at Spithead, at the Derby, Ascot and one of the England-Australia test matches. Some of these were no more than hardy annuals of the royal round, but many were silver jubilee extras. He was constantly at her side during drives, walkabouts and other celebrations in tourist-packed London, afterwards flying out with her to yet more Commonwealth countries – Canada, the Bahamas, Antigua, Barbados and the Virgin Isles. Silver jubilee travelling with Elizabeth resulted in him covering a total of about 7,000 miles in Britain and eight times more than that overseas. Yet he still managed to squeeze in a lot of additional mileage on his own account; another trip to Canada, visits to Afghanistan, Saudi Arabia, Algeria, Jamaica, Belgium and Monaco.

He was in as good a form as ever when making speeches, denouncing the planners – 'The effect of their operations has been to restrict individual initiative' – and speaking out against the permissive society: 'It is becoming only too apparent that it is possible for communities to achieve quite high standards of material development with, at the same time, the moral and behavioural standards of a colony of monkeys.' With the new micro-chip age just round the corner, he was far from supporting the view that industrial change was harsh and unfair. 'If you take that argument too far,' he argued, 'people would still be employed making bows and arrows, whalebone corsets, steam railway engines and antimacassars.'

Each speech, in turn, brought its quota of criticism – from politicians, bureaucrats, Trades Union bosses, left-wingers and do-gooders. Yet the fact was that Philip, as always, was simply putting into more elegant – and sometimes more witty – language what millions of ordinary people, company bosses and shop-floor workers alike, were saying in pubs and clubs, over dinner parties and darts games. As letters to national newspapers, in the aftermath of anti-Philip outbursts, put it again and again: . . . 'How right Prince Philip is.' . . : 'Prince Philip speaks for the majority of us.' . . . 'Prince Philip has put into words what the great majority of ordinary people feel.'

Postscript

It had become Earl Mountbatten's habit to spend a few weeks each summer at Classiebawn Castle, overlooking the tiny harbour of Mullaghmore in the Irish Republic. He was there as usual in the summer of 1979 and on 27 August he went out in his boat with members of his family to collect lobster pots. He was perhaps 440 yards out when the boat exploded, killing Mountbatten, his schoolboy grandson Nicholas and a young boatman, Paul Maxwell. It was the work of the IRA.

The murder of Earl Mountbatten, a few weeks after his seventy-ninth birthday, shocked not only Britain but the world. And if Britain had lost a man once described in Parliament as 'one of the truly great Englishmen of our time' – D-Day planner, the supremo who turned the tide of war against the Japanese in South-East Asia, last Viceroy of India – Philip, on a more personal level, had lost someone who stood almost in the relationship of a father to him. If it was Charles who was later publicly to denounce the 'mindless cruelty' of the 'sub-human extremists' who planted the bomb – he was speaking at a memorial service to the dead Earl in St Paul's cathedral – Philip's private comments were surely even more bitter and forthright. One can almost hear him saying, 'Bloody bastards', Mountbatten's death hit him hard. So hard, so deeply, that 'he seemed to age ten years almost overnight,' according to someone who saw him soon after. For a time the spring seemed to go out of his step and, for the first time, there was a stoop to the old poker-straight erectness.

But Philip is nothing if not tough and resilient. Within months he had bounced back and by December of that year he was in as good a voice as ever, castigating the 'appalling state' of Britain's bus stops, the 'ghastly mess' at railway stations and lambasting Heathrow as 'the most disastrous place you have ever seen.'

And so into the 1980s, gloomily prophesying (in yet another magazine interview) a world hit by poverty, starvation and disease, and finding himself, as president of the International Equestrian Federation*, caught up in the row over the Moscow Olympics which followed on the heels of the Soviet Union's invasion of Afghanistan. While so many British athletes might put their desire for transient glory ahead of the Government's wish to show the Soviets what the world thought of them, Philip, as Consort, could hardly do the same, even assuming he had any desire to do so. 'There is no way I can go to Moscow,' he said in Switzerland while attending a meeting of Olympic federations. 'That has been decided already by Parliament.' Because he is who he is, it was perhaps inevitable that the matter should not end there. Though he was in no way the motivator of the statement which emerged from that Swiss get-together denouncing the pressure Governments were putting on athletes to boycott the Moscow Games, it required an official statement from Buckingham Palace to nail the rumour that he was. 'It is totally untrue to suggest that the Duke of Edinburgh was in any way the motivator of the statement by the committee,' said a palace press officer. 'The Duke of Edinburgh used his best efforts to modify the statement, on which there was no vote. The Duke of Edinburgh has never personally criticised the position taken by the Government.'

Even before that particular rumpus Philip was in no doubt that it was a fallacy to suppose that international sport inevitably creates goodwill or that those taking part are always concerned more with participating than winning. 'Don't you believe it,' he told a meeting of the Recreation Managers' Association. 'So many countries see success as a means of gaining international prestige or as an advertisement for political theory or ideology

* Appendix IV.

[170]

that competition is simply a means to an end. They are not always so scrupulous about the means, either.'

And there, as a book must be printed if it is to be published, it is necessary to leave the life and times of Prince Philip. Neither are by any means over, but after more than twenty-five years as Consort it is possible to make some sort of valid and balanced assessment. Without doubt he has shaped his indefinable role as Consort in his own image; he has worked long and hard at giving it real shape and substance and there have been many achievements along the way.

It has been Philip more than anyone who has been responsible for hauling the Monarchy out of the Victorian atmosphere which still lingered at the outset of his wife's reign and placing it down firmly in the twentieth century. Or, at least as firmly as is possible without destroying the age-old traditions which make Monarchy what it is. It has been said of the Queen Mother that it was she who made a King of the nervous and uncertain man she married. The same cannot be said of Philip's relationship to the Queen. Elizabeth, despite the youthful age at which she succeeded to the throne, was always a Queen from the outset. But Philip has done much to mould and change her into the more contemporary and confident Queen of today. He has also ensured, by breaking with royal tradition and sending Charles to boarding school, by serving both as a model to him and a strong influence upon him, that it will be a very different King who will one day take over his mother's throne to what might have been. Through the multititudinous offices held during his years as Consort* he has changed British life in numerous small ways and many directions of which not everyone is aware. His one-time presidency of the Automobile Association, for instance, helped to bring about new road-safety measures, among them improved vehicle lighting, double white lines and crash helmets for motor-cyclists (though not all who ride motor bikes will thank him for that). Many lives may have been saved in consequence. His Duke of Edinburgh's Award scheme may equally have

* Appendix IV.

changed the lives of many youngsters, in other countries as well as Britain.

He has done his best, in the course of his world-wide travels, to bolster Britain's export trade. Because he does not go around with contracts tucked in his pocket, because – as he says himself – he can only 'create an atmosphere', it is impossible to prove, again, exactly how far he has succeeded. But there have been some obvious successes, as when a deal to supply Chile with its first nuclear reactor was completed, in the face of better financial terms from the French, after Philip had spoken out in Santiago about the benefits of trading with Britain.

At home, he has urged, exhorted, coerced and prodded his wife's subjects to work harder, the nation to pull up its industrial socks, businessmen to pull their fingers out, salesmen to sell more, and governments and planners to be less restrictive. Regrettably, in an era of marxist-inspired unrest resulting in strikes, go-slows, restrictive practices, poor workmanship and uncertain deliveries, no one seems to have been paying that much attention.

On a personal level, despite the anomaly of being married to a wife who does not bear his name and fathering children to whom his name is only a second-string, his marriage has been a happy one. If not exactly the fairy-tale love match of popular legend, neither was it an arranged match in the old Victorian sense and, on balance, things have worked out remarkably well. If the heady stuff of young love, when he once chased his young bride through their palace home in his pyjamas, has long since given way to the comfortable companionship that comes with the years, certainly husband and wife have neither bored each other nor find each other boring. Today, as always, in their moments together, they find plenty to talk about, their conversation broken at times by Elizabeth's throaty laughter (so seldom heard in public) and Philip's responding guffaw.

But suppose the two had never met; never married . . . what then? Marrying Elizabeth meant the sacrifice of Philip's naval career. The sacrifice may have come more quickly than he had anticipated, but sooner or later it had to come. While he is today

Admiral of the Fleet, that is simply a title, one of the several which adorn his role of Consort. What might have followed had he not married Elizabeth and not been compelled to abandon his naval career? His grandfather, Prince Louis of Battenberg, was First Sea Lord when he was so ungenerously hounded from office because of his German connections. His uncle, similarly, rose to become First Sea Lord and, when that role ceased to exist, ended an illustrious career as Chief of Staff to the Secretary of Defence and chairman of the Chief of Staffs Committee. True, it took a world war for both men to achieve greatness, Prince Louis in ensuring that the Royal Navy was in a sufficient state of readiness to meet the German threat when the First World War erupted and Earl Mountbatten in turning the tide of war against Japan during the Second World War.

Mountbatten went on to preside over the break-up of Britain's Indian Empire, a job he did not want and accepted only at the urging of George VI. 'You're the only man who can hope to pull it off,' the King said. If he did not succeed in pulling it off without bloodshed that was perhaps because it was the 'insoluble problem' he had always known it to be. He did his best and it was almost certainly more than any of his critics could have achieved.

Because he is Consort, the opportunity of emulating his uncle has been — and still is — denied to Philip. Anything even remotely political is out of reach. As Consort, he does not even have a vote. He is a member of the House of Lords, but sees no point in attending if he is hamstrung politically. Yet his speeches reveal a politically motivated man, forceful, articulate, imaginative.

A newspaper poll in 1969 invited newspaper readers to vote for the person they would most like to be president if Britain switched to the American system of presidential government. At that time neither Margaret Thatcher nor James Callaghan had yet achieved sufficient political stature to merit inclusion. So the main opposition came from Harold Wilson, Edward Heath and Enoch Powell. Only theoretically, of course, but all three notched fewer votes than Philip's thirteen per cent. However, a character named Don't Know did even better with forty-one per cent.

Philip was once asked, in that same *Director* interview which precipitated such a storm in Parliament, if he saw himself in 'some kind of leadership role'. He didn't, he said. 'People will respond to example more than direct leadership, I suspect. It sounds possibly rather idiotic, but I think I would rather influence people by example than by the type of commanding leadership you are suggesting.'

Yet headmaster Hahn saw Philip in boyhood as 'a born leader'. And to a born leader, surely, example and influence must seem but pale substitutes for power and authority. So did he mean it? Or was it a diplomatically appropriate answer dictated by the fact that he is who he is?

Hahn also saw Philip as requiring 'the exacting demands of a great service' if he was to do full justice to himself. 'His best is outstanding,' Hahn wrote. 'His second best is not good enough.'

That Philip has worked long, hard and conscientiously in his role of Consort, few will deny. Even Willie Hamilton, no lover of Monarchy, once conceded as much. The role is undeniably an exacting one, but with all its limitations, restrictions and frustrations, is it a sufficiently 'great service', or enough of a challenge, to have sparked the outstanding best of which Hahn thought him capable? Only Philip himself can know the answer to that one.

THE DANISH CONNECTION

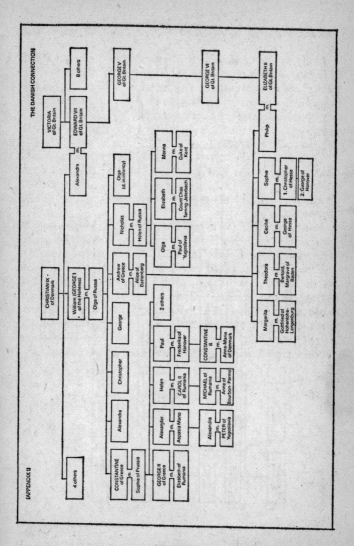

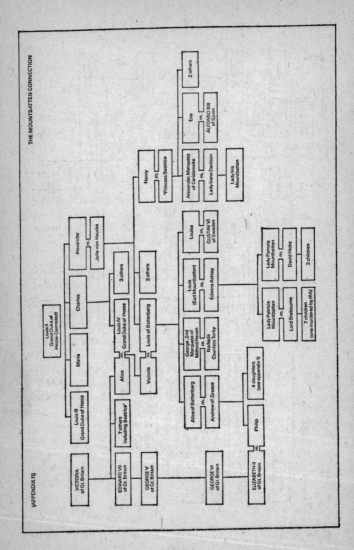

THE MOUNTBATTEN CONNECTION

(APPENDIX II)

Appendix III

Prince Philip's Travels

Year	On his own	With the Queen
1950	Middle East, Turkey, Gibraltar, plus courtesy calls on King Ibn Saud and King Abdullah of Jordan (while in Navy)	Greece, Libya (The Queen was still Princess Elizabeth)
1951		Italy, Canada, USA
1952	Finland, Norway, Sweden, France, Malta	Kenya (en route to Australia and New Zealand when King George VI died)
1953	West Germany*	Bermuda, Jamaica, Fiji, Tonga, New Zealand, Australia, Ceylon, Uganda, Malta, Libya, Gibraltar
1954	France, West Germany,* Canada	
1955	Malta and the Mediterranean, West Germany (twice),* Denmark	Norway

1956–1957	Mediterranean and Gibraltar, Seychelles, Ceylon, Papua New Guinea, Malaya, Australia, New Zealand, Chatham Island, Deception Island, South Shetlands, Falkland Islands, Tristan da Cunha, St Helena, Ascension Island, Gambia, Gibraltar, West Germany*	Nigeria, Sweden, Portugal, France, Denmark, Canada, USA
1958	West Germany (twice),* Belgium, Canada	Netherlands
1959	India, Pakistan, Singapore, Sarawak, North Borneo, Hong Kong, Solomon Islands, Gilbert and Ellice Islands, Christmas Island, Bahamas, Bermuda, Ghana	Canada, USA
1960	Malta, Switzerland, West Germany,* Canada, USA	
1961	West Germany,* Tanganyika	Cyprus, India, Pakistan, Nepal, Iran, Turkey, Italy and the Vatican, Ghana, Liberia, Sierra Leone and Gambia
1962	British Guiana, Venezuela, Colombia, Ecuador, Peru, Bolivia, Chile, Paraguay, Uruguay, Brazil, Argentina, Canada (twice), USA (twice),	Netherlands (semi-private)

1962 cont.	Australia, Italy (private), West Germany*	
1963	USA, Kenya (private), Zanzibar, Sudan	Australia, New Zealand, Fiji, Canada
1964	Greece (twice), Iceland, Malawi, Malta, Mexico, Galapagos Islands, Panama, Trinidad and Tobago, Grenada, St Vincent, Barbados, St Lucia, Dominica, St Kitts, Montserrat, Antigua, West Germany,* France, Belgium, Morocco	Canada
1965	Saudi Arabia, Pakistan (twice), India, Singapore, Australia, Sarawak, Brunei, Sabah, Malaya, Thailand, Nepal, Bahrain, Greece, Italy (twice), France (twice), West Germany, Switzerland, Belgium	Ethiopia, Sudan, West Germany
1966	USA, Canada, Netherlands, Norway, West Germany,* Jamaica, Argentina, Monaco, Italy, France	Guyana, Trinidad, Tobago, Grenada, St Vincent, Barbados, St Lucia, Dominica, Montserrat, Antigua, St Kitts-Nevis-Anguilla, Virgin Islands, Turks and Caicos Islands, Bahamas, Jamaica, Belgium

1967	Iran, Australia, France (twice), Netherlands, Italy, Canada (twice)	Canada, West Germany, Malta
1968	Oman, Jaipur, Malaysia, Indonesia, Thailand, Bali, Australia, New Zealand, Singapore, Malta, Mexico	Brazil, Chile, Senegal
1969	Ethiopia, Kenya (semi-private), France, West Germany, Canada, USA, Switzerland	Austria, Norway (unofficial)
1970	France, USA, Finland, Italy, West Germany (twice), Belgium	Fiji, Tonga, New Zealand, Australia, Canada
1971	Galapagos Islands, Easter Island, Pitcairn Island, Cook Island, Samoa, Fiji, New Hebrides, Solomon Islands, Bougainville, New Guinea, Australia, West Germany (twice),* France, Hungary, Iran, Sweden	Canada, Turkey
1972	Denmark, Kenya, West Germany (four times, one private), Liechtenstein (private), Holland (private), Belgium	Thailand, Singapore, Malaysia, Brunei, Maldive Islands, Seychelles, Mauritius, Kenya, France, Yugoslavia
1973	Hungary, Yugoslavia, Iran,	Canada (twice), Australia

1973 *cont.*	Afghanistan, India, Thailand, Singapore, Australia (twice), West Germany,* Portugal, Denmark, Soviet Union, Sweden, Bulgaria, New Zealand, Belgium, Luxembourg (private)	
1974	New Zealand, Australia, France (twice), Switzerland (twice), West Germany (twice, one private), Austria (private), Canada, USA, Belgium	Cook Islands, New Zealand, Norfolk Island, New Hebrides, Solomon Islands, Papua New Guinea, Singapore, Indonesia
1975	Belize, El Salavador, Honduras, Costa Rica, St Lucia, Grand Turk Island, Poland, Morocco, Netherlands, West Germany,* Spain, Belgium	Bermuda, Barbados, Bahamas, Jamaica, Mexico, Hawaii, Hong Kong, Japan
1976	Liechtenstein (private), Canada, Netherlands, Mexico, West Germany (twice, one private), Belgium	Canada, USA, Finland, Luxembourg
1977	Afghanistan, Saudi Arabia, Monaco, Algeria, West Germany (private), Canada, Jamaica, Belgium	West Samoa, Tonga, Fiji, New Zealand, Australia, Papua New Guinea, Canada, Bahamas, West Plana Cay (private), Little Inagua (private), Virgin Islands,

1977 *cont.*		Antigua, Mustique (private), Barbados
1978	Canada (three times), Liechtenstein (private), Luxembourg (private), West Germany (four times, one private), Hungary, USA (three times), Puerto Rico, France	Canada, West Germany
1979	France (twice, one private), Oman, Soviet Union, West Germany (three times, one private), Sweden (twice), Netherlands (twice), Denmark, Australia, Switzerland, Lichtenstein (private), Canada, Luxembourg (private)	Kuwait, Bahrain, Saudi Arabia, Oman, Qatar, United Arab Emirates, Denmark, Tanzania, Botswana, Malawi, Zambia

* Frequent West German visits mainly to visit British forces.

Appendix IV

Appointments, Presidencies etc.

The following are among the more important posts Prince Philip holds or has held during his years as Consort.

APPOINTMENTS: Admiral, Sea Cadet Corps (from · 1952), Colonel-in-Chief, Army Cadet Force (from 1952), Air Commodore-in-Chief, Air Training Corps (from 1952), Captain General, Royal Marines (from 1953), Colonel-in-Chief, Queen's Royal Irish Hussars (from 1958), Duke of Edinburgh's Royal Regiment (from 1959), Queen's Own Highlanders (from 1961), Royal Electrical and Mechanical Engineers (from 1969), Intelligence Corps (from 1977); Colonel, Welsh Guards (1953–75), Grenadier Guards (from 1975).

PRESIDENCIES: Air League (for 1969), Association of Technical Institutions (1964–6), Australian Conservation Foundation (1971–6), Automobile Association (1951–61), British Amateur Athletic Board (from 1952), British Association for the Advancement of Science (1951–3), British Commonwealth Ex-Services League (from 1974), British Crafts Centre (1972–5), British Horse Society (for 1956, Vice-President 1957–67), British Medical Association (1959–60), British Racing Drivers Club (from 1952), British Sportsman's Club (from 1958), British Sub-Aqua Club (1960–63), Canadian Medical Association (1959–60), Central Council of Physical Recreation (from 1951), Cheam School Association (1952–72), City and Guilds of London Institute (from 1951), Coal Trade Benevolent Association (from 1976), Commonwealth Games Federation (from 1955), Company of Veteran Motorists (1959–62), Cornish Cricket Society (1961–2), Council of Engineering Institutions (1965–75), Council of Trustees of the Air Centre (1968–73), Council for National Academic Awards (1965–75), Council for Volunteers Overseas (1964–8), Crafts Centre of Great Britain (1952–64, 1967–72), Crafts Council of Great Britain (1964–9), Duke of Edinburgh's Study Conference (from 1972), English Association (1967–8), English-Speaking Union of the Commonwealth (from 1952), Federation Equestre Internationale (1964–76), Football Association (1955–8), Uffa Fox Memorial Community Centre and Nautical Museum (from 1974), Friends of Malta, G.C. (1965–7), Game Conservancy (1964–73), Guards Polo Club (from 1955), Guinea Pig Club (from 1960), Hackney Horse Society (for 1977), Helicopter Club of Great Britain (1968–71), Highland Society of London (1962–3), Historic Churches Preservation Trust (from 1952), Institute of Marine Engineers (1962–3), Institute of Mathematics (for 1976 and 1977), Institute of Sports Medicine (1967–70), Institute of Practitioners in Work Study (1975–7), Institution of Highway Engineers (1960–1), International Lawn Tennis Club of Great Britain (1962–5), Licensed Victuallers' National Homes (for 1966 and 1974), Lord's Taverners (for 1960 and 1961), Maritime Trust (1969–79), Marylebone Cricket Club (for 1949, 1974–5), Medical Commission on Accident Prevention (1968–72). Missions to Seamen (1956–7), National Association of Industries for the Blind and Disabled (1972–5), National Book League (1963–71), National Council of Social Service (1970–3), National Federation of Housing Associations (1975–80), National Federation of Parent-Teachers' Associations (1960–5), National Federation of Young Farmers' Clubs (1961–4), National Playing Fields Association (1949–78), Printers' Pension, Almhouse and Orphan Asylum Corporation (for 1963, life Vice-President since), Royal Aero Club (1964–71), Royal Agricultural Society of England (for 1957 and 1963), Royal Agricultural Society of the Commonwealth (from 1958), Royal Air Forces Association (1967–9), Royal Association of British Dairy Farmers (for 1957, 1965, 1973–5), Royal Caledonian

Curling Club (1964–5), Royal College of General Practitioners (1972–3), Royal Household Cricket Club (from 1953), Royal Merchant Navy School (from 1952), Royal Microscopical Society (for 1966), Royal Mint Advisory Committee (from 1952), Royal Postgraduate Medical School (1975–8), Royal Smithfield Club (for 1972, Vice President from 1971), Royal Society of Arts (from 1952), Royal Society for the Prevention of Accidents (1966–8), Royal Yachting Association (1956–70 1975–7), Schools Science and Technology Committee Standing Conference (1971–6), Scottish-Icelandic Association (from 1965), Smeatonian Society of Civil Engineers (for 1971), Society for Underwater Technology (1974–6), Society of Film and TV Arts (1958–65), Society of the Friends of St George (from 1948), Spastics Society (1957–65), Technician Education Council (1975–80), Westminister Abbey Trust (1972–7), Wildfowl Trust (1960–5, 1972–7), World Wildlife Fund, British National Appeal (from 1961), Zoological Society of London (1960–77).

CHANCELLORSHIPS: Cambridge University (from 1976), Edinburgh University (from 1952), Salford University (1967–77), Wales University (from 1948).

COMMONWEALTH APPOINTMENTS: Field Marshal, Admiral of the Fleet and Marshal of the Royal Australian Air Force (from 1954);Colonel-in-Chief, Royal Australian Electrical and Mechanical Engineers (from 1959), Australian Cadet Corps (from 1963); Colonel-in-Chief, Royal Canadian Regiment (from 1953), Royal Canadian Army Cadets (from 1953), Seaforth Highlanders (from 1967), Cameron Highlanders of Ottawa (from 1967), Queen's Own Cameron Highlanders (from 1967), Royal Hamilton Light Infantry (from 1978); Admiral, Royal Canadian Sea Cadets (from 1953), Air Commodore-in-Chief, Royal Canadian Air Cadets (from 1953); Privy Councillor (from 1957); Admiral of the Fleet, New Zealand (from 1958), Colonel-in-Chief, Royal New Zealand Electrical and Mechanical Engineers (from 1970), Field Marshal and Marshal of the Royal New Zealand Air Force (from 1977).

USA APPOINTMENTS: Hon. Member, Honourable Artillery Company of Massachusetts (from 1952); Admiral, Great Navy of the State of Nebraska (from 1958); Honorary Colonel, Honourable Order of Kentucky Colonels (from 1967), Confederate Air Force of Harlingen, Texas (from 1976); Honorary Deputy Sheriff, Los Angeles County (from 1966); Grand Commander, San Francisco Port Authority (from 1968).

Believe it or not, there are more; to many to list here and enough to justify an entry in the Guiness Book of Records.

Bibliography

QUEEN ALEXANDRA OF YUGOSLAVIA, *Prince Philip, A Family Portrait* (Hodder & Stoughton, 1960)

RAY BELLISARIO, *To Tread On Royal Toes* (Impulse Publications Ltd 1972)

BASIL BOOTHROYD, *Philip, An Informal Biography* (Longman)

DIARIES OF SIR HENRY CHANNON, *Chips* (Weidenfeld & Nicholson, 1967)

PRINCE CHRISTOPHER OF GREECE, *Memoirs* (Hurst & Blackett, 1938)

HELENE CORDET, *Born Bewildered* (Peter Davies, 1961)

MARION CRAWFORD, *The Little Princesses* (Cassell & Co 1950)

MARION CRAWFORD, *Queen Elizabeth II* (George Newnes, 1952)

JOHN DEAN, *HRH Prince Philip* (Robert Hale)

ALDEN HATCH, *The Mountbattens* (W. H. Allen)

SIR LESLIE HOLLIS, *The Captain General* (Herbert Jenkins, 1961)

PRINCE NICHOLAS OF GREECE, *My Fifty Years* (Hutchinson)

L. A. NICKOLLS, *The Queen's World Tour* (Macdonald & Co)

(SELECTED SPEECHES 1956–9) *Prince Philip Speaks* (Collins)

JOHN TERRAINE, *The Life and Times of Lord Mountbatten* (Hutchinson & Co)

LOUIS WULFF, *Elizabeth & Philip* (Sampson Low 1947)

Index

Philip, Prince
ancestry 23, 174–6, appearance 11, appointments 8, 65, 96, 183–6, arts patron 17–18, betrothal 9, 63–4, bird-watching 157, birth 25, (and) *Britannia* 106–7, (and) Buckingham Palace 94–5, 98–100, 139–40, carriage driving 152–3, character 11, 13, 17, 18, 19–21, 35, 36, 39, 42, 45, 57, 66, 74, 76, 82, 87, 107, 110, 131, 137–8, childhood 28–31, 33–4, (as) Consort 10–11, 14–15, 19–20, 91–3, 104–5, 108, 125–6, 127–8, 129–30, 132, 134–5, 166–8, 171–2, (and) coronation 104–5, courtship 48, 50, 51, 55–6, criticisms of 15, 17, 98, 138–9, 160–1, 162–3, 164, 168, (at) Dartmouth 41–3, designer 17, Duke of Edinburgh's Award 117–18, education 7, 29–31, 32–7, (as) father 21, 79–80, 83, 101, 113–15, 126–7, 136–7, 141–2, 145–7, 153, finances 72, 75, 81–2, 96, 148–9, 150–1, 164–6, first meeting with Elizabeth 41–3, flying 37, 102–4, 156, frustrations 94–6, (and) girls 38, 46, 49, habits 12, health 13, 76, 96, 152, height 7, 11, honeymoon 71, 72, (as) husband 21, 74, 172, (and) King George VI 74, 88–9, 89–90, married life 72–5, 97, 113, (and) Moscow Olympics 170, mother – see Alice, Princess, (and) Mountbatten, Earl, 37–8, 169, name 60–1, National Playing Fields Association 80–1, 84, naturalization 8, 9, 60, 61–2, naval career 7–8, 39, 44–9, 50–1, 52–3, 54, 55, 75, 81–5, painting 157–8, photography 15, 120, (and) photographers 66, 76–7, 138, 153–4, (and) politics 15, 16, 144–5, 160–3, polo 82, 83, 104, 131, 141, 152, popularity 11, 109, 166, (and) press 16, 60, 67, 116, 122, 155–6, (and) Queen Mother 74, 137, rift rumour 116, 121–4, sailing 101–2, 140–1, (and) Sandringham 100–1, schooldays – *see* education, sensitivity 17–18, 143–4, 169, (and) silver jubilee 164, 166–8, silver wedding 154, shooting 58, 59, 88, 138–9, (and) smoking 12–13, speeches 16–17, 65, 84–5, 97–8, 127, 144, 148–9, 159–60, 168, 170, sport (in schooldays) 33, 34, 35–6, sport (in navy) 42, 82, 83, 84, (and) television 15–16, 127–8, 147–8, titles 8, 10–11, 69, 96, 124, travels 12, 13, 76, 83, 84, 86–8, 107–10, 110–11, 117–21, 128–9, 133, 134–5, 139, 143, 145, 148–9, 158–9, 166, 168, 177–82, wedding 67–70, (and) Windsor Castle 95, 101, 112–13, wit 18–19, 66–7, 68, 79, 98, 109, 167, workload 11, 13, 81, 97, 104, 156, 166–8, Second World War 44–53

Phillips, Mark 136, 154–6, 159